Donations to Dollars!

Maximizing In-Kind Donations for Non-Profits

And Multiple Streams of Revenue

By Stacie Morrell

Contents

Introduction

One of the primary issues facing non-profit organizations is finding stable, sustainable streams of revenue. Not everyone wanting to support your organization and its mission have time to volunteer or money to donate, but nearly everyone has 'stuff.'

This book will guide your organization to bountiful donations of 'stuff' or 'used goods' (properly known as in-kind donations), and how to maximize the value of those items to support your mission.

Those in-kind donations can be turned into cash for your cause. If your dedicated donors are passing along their previously valued items, you owe it to your mission, donors, volunteers, employees, and board to realize the most revenue from those items as possible.

This book is not intended to make you an expert in all things collectible or antique but to give you a basic understanding of what to look for. It is intended to educate on the ways of the resale and secondary markets and all the streams of revenue therein. It is also intended to help your organization think outside the box for fundraising and in-kind donations.

This guide will teach you:

- How to recruit in kind donations
- How to sell used good donations to maximize their value
- How to recruit volunteers to do the above
- How to determine what items are worth more than average
- How to develop multiple streams of revenue from in-kind donations

Let's start at the beginning and assume you are starting from the ground up.

Chapter 1

First, your organization needs to **build your donor base** –

In order to maximize donations, your organization needs to acquire donations. You should already have a donor base for cash and event donations. Now you need to spread the word about accepting in-kind donations.

I would advise against taking large furniture. It sells slowly and takes up a lot of valuable room. Instead, partner with the nearest Habitat for Humanity Re-Store or similar organization. You can send them furniture donations; they can send you small item donations. You will lend them volunteers for urgent needs if they lend you volunteers for issues such as picking up large donations (estates, garage sale leftovers, rummage sale leftovers) and they can have the furniture from the contact you made in exchange for their help and vice versa.

Social media is essential for spreading the word. Use it liberally. You organization should already have a Facebook page. Post to it and share to groups related to your mission and local community news and buy/sell groups.

https://www.facebook.com/fundraisers/
https://www.facebook.com/marketplace/

Do you have a mailing list of past and current donors? You should. Send out an email announcing the need for in-kind donations.

Need a nonprofit database? I like DonorPerfect but here are some choices:
https://www.softwareadvice.com/nonprofit/
https://www.capterra.com/nonprofit-software/
https://www.qgiv.com/blog/top-nonprofit-software/

Or go with an email marketing company:
https://www.constantcontact.com/index.jsp
https://mailchimp.com/

Get your executive director on the local radio station for an interview or just a simple announcement.

Get the local newspaper to do a story on your organization.

Have volunteers hand out flyers asking for leftovers at garage sales, rummage sales, estate sales, flea markets, church bazars, etc.

While you are spreading the word about accepting donations, don't forget to recruit volunteers to sort, price, haul, etc. Recruit volunteers with large vehicles (trucks, SUVs, trailers) to pick up donations. Recruit people to sort and price the items when they come in.

Here is an example of what I do when at an estate or garage sale:
- I walk in like a customer and look around.
- Smile, greet people, be pleasant.
- I determine if there are enough items we would want for it to be worth taking everything that may be leftover.
- It always helps if you buy something, which never seems to be a problem for me.
- Greet the people running the sale and have a business card or flyer ready.
  - "Hi! I'm from (insert your organization's name here) and we (have an elevator pitch ready 30 seconds or less, and outline what it is your organization does) We would love

to receive your leftovers after your
sale for our thrift store/rummage sale.
Would you consider donating to us?
We give tax receipts for donations. We
are a 501c3 organization."

- If you can pick up the items, then you are
ahead of 90% of the nonprofit organizations
out there and that is a big bonus incentive
for your donors.
- Thank them warmly and tell them to have a
great day, even if they don't seem like they
will donate. A positive attitude has won me
many donors over the years, just by being
nice and friendly.

USEFUL TIP: Look on Facebook and Craigslist
for local garage/rummage sales. Post a comment
on Facebook posts asking for leftovers. Tag the
posting person so they see it in their notifications.
Don't forget to include your address and hours of
operation and what the donations will benefit.

**Here is an example of an effective flyer I take to
sales with me:**

MAKE A DONATION

Your Organization or Thrift Store Name

Your store or donation drop off location

Hours: Your drop off or store hours

We gladly accept:

Lamps	Décor
Books	Pets Items
Kitchen Items	Records/CDs/DVDs
Glassware	Small Furniture
Porcelain/Pottery	Purses/Bags
Puzzles/Games	Clothing
Jewelry	Tools
Crafting	Electrical
Sports Items	Toys

WE PICK-UP!

Call for more information: Store number

Proceeds benefit (Your organization here)

Chapter 2

You are now receiving, sorting, and storing donations. As you sort, you should be looking for higher end items. Those are items that are collectible, designer, high priced new, such as electronics, or valuable such as fine jewelry.

You should sort those higher value items into a separate area and take them to be listed online, sent to auction, taken to consignment, etc.

If you are doing rummage sales combined with internet sales, you will need an office with shelves for storage and a packing area and internet connection in addition to the storage unit.

Perhaps you have access to a box truck for free and long-term use. Fill it with donations until it's full, then have a rummage sale. Do this until you can expand to a larger space.

OR start with a large, dry, enclosed space. Minimum should be about the size of a large storage space or 2 large offices, one to store and one to sort. They should be ground level; trust me, you don't want it to involve stairs in any way.

Or you can rent a storage unit. If you have access to free space, use it. If you don't, then shop around for storage companies that offer non-profit discounts.

Not all donations are worthy of keeping. There will be items in poor condition and broken items. To save space in your storage area, you can presort the items when they are received, casting off the items unworthy of further attention.

You can stockpile for a rummage sale (or for opening a thrift store if you're ready.)
*Start at the back wall with a line of boxes, each for a different department (i.e. books/media, clothing, glass/pottery/porcelain, décor, etc.)
*When a box gets full, close it up and stack an empty one on top .
*Continue up until it's chest high (and you can't reach anymore) and then start a new stack in front of the full one.
*When you finish, you will have a wall of boxes, pre-sorted, for your upcoming sale(s).
*Label each box in case things get chaotic while transporting and setting up. *You can tag items as you sort, or tag them when you set up, or decide to have a flat price for each category

(books, glass/porcelain, kitchen, toys, etc.) and just make signs with the prices.

Below is an example of a rummage sale pricing sign I have used in the past. Feel free to adjust the prices for your clientele. I am assuming you have taken out higher value and special items. If you are not selling items online, price the higher end items at half what they are selling for online. Individually price large items like sets and doll houses.

For dishes, kitchen utensils and pots/pans, only offer the ones in good useable condition. Do not put out pans with chipping non-stick coating or burn stains or loose handles, etc. Only price the plastic containers that are not stains or scratched or made to throw away/recycle.

Fishing rods should be looked up by brand, some are better than others and could have good resale value. Skate boards are usually abused but can still sell for parts at $5.00. Research any that are like new or barely used. Fishing tackle can be sold in lots for $3.00-5.00, but if it's still in the package or vintage, research it.

These prices work for a thrift store as well. Adjust up for quality and brand or upscale area. Don't put out broken, incomplete or worn out items.

Toys:	.25 small .50-1.00 larger or plush
Dolls:	1.00
Games:	1.00 card 2.00 board
Books:	paperback .50 hardback 1.00
Audio books:	1.00 cassette 2.00 CD
Framed Art:	3.00 large 2.00 medium 1.00 small
Frames	.25 small .50 medium 1.00 large
Glass/Pottery/Porcelain:	.50 small 1.00 medium 2.00 large
Records:	.50
CDs:	1.00
DVDs:	2.00 single 4.00 sets/series
CD/DVDVHS Racks:	3.00-5.00
Cassettes:	.25
Kitchen utensils:	.50
Small Appliances:	5.00-10.00
Pots & Pans:	2.00-5.00
Tupperware:	1.00-3.00
Other plastic containers:	.25-1.00
Flatware:	.25
Clothes:	Kid's 1.00 Shirts 2.00 Pants 3.00 Leggings 2.00
Shoes:	2.00 kid 4.00 adult Boots 5.00

Accessories: .50

Jewelry: .50-1.00

Small knick knacks 1.00

Linen: .50

Computer Games: 2.00

System Games (PS, Wii, etc.) 3.00

Cords/Chargers/Remotes 1.00

Holiday: Lights 2.00

Ornaments 1.00

Tree stands 5.00

Tree toppers 3.00

Tools: .50 small 1.00 medium

large 2.00

Power Tools: 5.00-10.00

Bicycles: 5.00 Kid 10.00 youth

20.00 adult

Sports equipment: Individually marked

Pet Supplies: .25 cat toys .50 dog toys 1.00 collars 2.00 leashes 1.00 dishes & misc.

Unless individually marked.

Minimum needed for rummage sales:

- Volunteers – to load, unload, tag, carry, display, cashier, etc.
- Truck(s) – Volunteers or talk to your storage place, they sometimes have trucks for renters.

- Tables – Talk to churches or organizations such as American Legion, Elks, Rotary, etc., about borrowing items they may have.
- Price tags - Dollar Store!
- Pens – Dollar Store!
- Signs – Volunteers can make them and supplies can be found at the Dollar Store.
- Stapler and staples to put up signs (You may even get pens, staples and a stapler donated…)
- Cash box – for all that money you're going to make.
- Cash - $100 total consisting of 1's= $40, 5's= $50, and $10 roll of quarters to make change.
- Bags – paper, plastic, whatever you can round up.

How to have a successful rummage sale:
- ✓ Don't bother with pricing anything less than .25 to make change and calculations easier.
- ✓ Try to choose times when the weather is not blistering hot or sopping wet and avoid holiday weekends.
- ✓ Fridays and Saturdays are best.
- ✓ Start your sale no later than 9am. Afternoons are slow, so end around 3pm or

4pm so you have time to clean up before it gets too late.

Divide the tasks! You should have 1-2 people for each of the following jobs to avoid burn out of your volunteers.

- Signage and advertising
- Tables, transportation of items
- Setting up
- Cashier and bagging (responsible for gathering lots of bags & wrapping)
- Clean up of leftover items and tables
- Taking signs down
- Banking – The Executive Director, bookkeeper, or Donation Manager should do this.

Place an advertisement for the sale TWO WEEKS before the sale, to give people time to see the ads and plan their time. Places to advertise:

- Local newspaper(s)
- Facebook
- Craigslist
- https://nextdoor.com/find-neighborhood/

SIGNS

- ✓ Signs should be about 12x18" but check with your town/city sign ordinance to see what limits there are.
- ✓ In large black block letters (get the biggest marker you can find) write RUMMAGE SALE, days and times, street address, and an arrow pointing in the direction the driver should go. As a garage sale enthusiast, I find this really helpful.
- ✓ Make all lettering large and the same size. Customers need to read this while driving.
- ✓ Get your signage at the dollar store; they have corrugated plastic or poster board and metal sign brackets to stick in the ground you can attach your sign to.
- ✓ Place signs at the busiest intersections and any turn the customers must make to get to you. Don't skimp on signage.

You need to decide if you will accept cash only or credit cards as well.

If you do, you will need a smart phone, tablet or laptop and a payment account such as PayPal or Square or Google payments. If you already have a credit card processing account set up with a bank or company, contact them about accepting payments at your sale. Due to fees, it is necessary to have a minimum for credit/debit sales. I usually go with $5.00.

For PayPal: Your customer can forward payment to your PayPal account. Just give them the total and your email for your PayPal account. Notification of the payment will come to you and your customer via email. To sign up https://www.paypal.com/us/webapps/mpp/account -selection

For Square: https://squareup.com/us/en/payments Square is easy to use, offers many functions and services, and is currently among the cheapest services for payments. You can use an iPad or other smart tablet, which can be purchased on EBay or Craigslist for about $100-$150 depending on your desired features:

When you set up, put the emptied boxes under the tables so customers can use them and they will be available for packing up at the end.

Set up the cashier table where customers enter/exit. Keep your cash box on a small table or chair behind the check-out table so it can't be grabbed or dipped into. Make the isles wide enough for 2 people to pass comfortably, and the isles 'flow' in an organized pattern, so people end up back at the cashier table, and items are arranged by type in sections.

For your leftover items, look on Craigslist and Facebook for people who will come and take the stuff away, or take it to another thrift charity such as Goodwill or St. Vincent's or Salvation Army, etc.

Items you should avoid taking or selling entirely:

- ☐ Large furniture (slow selling and takes up too much space, the exception being bookcases and dressers/chest of drawers. They sell! Also, antique of vintage items are desirable and bring better money so they will usually earn their keep. Avoid china cabinets and buffets. They don't sell. People don't use formal china much anymore and large buffets likewise.)
- ☐ Children's clothes with drawstrings (Banned by the Consumer Safety Department)
- ☐ Hair Dryers (safety issue)
- ☐ Hair Curlers (safety issue unless they look unused)
- ☐ Cribs (safety issues)
- ☐ Playpens/play yards (safety issues)
- ☐ Infant and toddler car seats and carriers (safety issues)
- ☐ Infant swings (safety issues)
- ☐ Bean bag chairs (just one time of beans all over the place and you'll understand why)

☐   <u>Lawn darts</u> (banned by the Consumer Safety Department)

☐   <u>Mattresses</u> (sanitary issues)

☐   <u>Used underwear</u> (socks in good condition and bras in nearly new condition are fine)

Resale consumer safety guides:

https://www.cpsc.gov/s3fs-public/ResellersGuide.pdf

Chapter 3

Thanking your donors is essential to <u>retaining</u> your donors. For donations that are significant, I would say $500 value or greater, a personal letter of thanks from the executive director or manager of in-kind donations is warranted.

It's important to show donors what their donation is doing, weather it is cash, volunteering or in-kind donations.

That brings us to another important point: don't forget to thank your volunteers! Discounts of services or in your thrift store, birthday cards, Christmas cards, yearend thank you letters, yearly volunteer picnic or dinner, pick at least 2 or 3 ways to thank your volunteers because you can never thank them enough and they are essential to the success of your organization.

End of year form letters of thanks should go out in December or January. Donors appreciate this as they may have lost their donation slips when the original donation was made, and it also serves to remind them of your existence in time for Christmas and year-end cleaning out.

Example letter of thanks:

Gift Date:
Gift Type: (Check, cash or in-kind)
Amount or Fair Market Value:

Name and address
Of donor

<u>Donor's first name</u>, you have made our shelter animal's day with your generous donation. Homeward Bound Pets is Oregon's 1st no-kill shelter since 1975 and continue that practice today. We are proud to say that we rescued and found forever homes for 545 dogs and cats in 2018. Your funds will be used to:

- Save the lives of surrendered, abandoned and homeless animals
- Purchase canned and dry food for our cats and dogs
- Keep our animals cool in the summer, warm and dry in the winter
- Make sure all adoptable animals are spayed or neutered, get the necessary tests, vaccines and veterinarian care needed
- Have knowledgeable, caring and loving people look after our shelter animals until we can find them their forever homes.

HBPets is celebrating 44 years in Yamhill County this year and with your generous donation we will continue to help those without a voice.

- 🐾 Remember Homeward Bound Pets when planning your estate
- 🐾 Become a "Friend of HBPets" by donating monthly by sending your donation through the mail to HBPets at PO Box 8, McMinnville, OR 97128 or by credit card on our website at hbpets.org.
- 🐾 Become a temporary Foster Parent for a puppy, dog, cat or kitten

Donations are essential to all our operations and your support for our work is valued and appreciated. Your donation may qualify for an IRS income tax deduction. (Federal Tax ID # 93-0687293). No goods or services were provided to the donor in consideration for this contribution.

_____

Signature and title of Organization Representative Include your contact information!

https://www.frontstream.com/blog/donation-thank-you-letters

https://www.template.net/business/letters/sample-donation-thank-you-letter/

Chapter 4

The key to maximizing your in-kind donations is multiple streams of revenue. That means market your stuff in more than one venue. To do this accurately and effectively, your organization should have a dedicated donations and online team. It can begin with one or two volunteers, but build your team early, so there is momentum and organization behind your in-kind donation management.

The more streams of revenue you have, the more revenue. Start with the obvious collectibles and selling sites, and branch out from there as you gain knowledge and volunteers or start earning enough to hire an employee to manage or coordinate the multiple selling venues and items.

Here are options to consider:
·   Online
·   Consignment
·   Auctions (for quality/higher value items)
·   Rummage sales (yearly, bi-yearly, quarterly)
·   Combination of all of the above

There are quite a few opportunities to market your items in your community.

Auctions – If there is an auction house within a reasonable distance, look at their website or contact them regarding what items they take. Every one is different due to location, etc.
https://www.liveauctioneers.com
Proxybid.com
Or do a Google search for 'auctions near me.'
Consignment is a way to maximize your nicer quality or designer items and develop multiple streams of revenue.

How consignment shops work:
Every shop has a list of what they take and do not take. Go to their website or into their store and ask for the consignment policies or contract. Review these fully. They will tell you what they want, don't want, how much they pay, etc. Some give you a choice to pick up items that don't sell. If you have time, get the unsold items. If you don't just let the consignment store give them to whoever they wish.

For very nice like new or vintage items, consignment stores may bring you more than a rummage sale or your thrift store. Take a clear picture of the item and ask if they would take it for consignment and how much they would put on it. Then take off the percentage they will keep and see if it's more than you could get on your own.

Items to consider for a consignment store are:
· Like new or expensive toys
· Designer, signed or quality jewelry
· Designer and like new clothing
· Like new shoes
· Designer or like new purses, bags, backpacks
· Like new furniture

Most nonprofits who accept clothing get overwhelmed with it. The best strategy for smaller non-profits is to sort the items as they come in. Store the off season clothing. Consignment stores won't take them off season and you can sell them for more during the correct season. Then, take the designer items and items in excellent condition to the consignment store. Most have you wait while they choose what they will take and then give you back what they don't. Make sure they want the larger items before transporting them. This results in 2 streams of revenue!

Bookstores – Sellers of used books buy used books. Often they will only give you trade, but some bookstores pay cash. Find out what kinds of books they want. Take clean, intact and good looking books to them in the subjects or authors they are looking for. Most thrift stores sell their books for 1-2.00 for hardbacks and .50-1.00 for paperbacks, so chances are you will get more selling them to a bookstore, unless they are selling for 6.00 or more on Amazon not including shipping. More on that later.

Music stores – The criteria and process for books also applies to most music stores that purchase used items, such as CDs and cassettes or music memorabilia. Many music stores also carry music-centric items and collectibles. Compare the prices the music store will pay to what you could get online or in your store or rummage sale.

Jewelry Stores – Find a reputable jeweler and build a relationship. That way, when you have fine jewelry come in (vs costume jewelry, which is not made of real gems or precious metals) you can have the stones identified and metal tested for gold or silver content. Many independent jewelry stores take consignment, so if it's a very nice piece it would probably pay to consign it. Or you can sell gold for fast cash by weight. Silver, currently, is bringing very little per gram, so it is more profitable to sell the sterling and 800 pieces in your store or online. Some jewelry stores don't take costume or silver items, some do, so be sure to compare and ask.

Antique Malls – If you have items that are nice but only range in value from $5-10 then perhaps a small space or case in an antique mall might work for you. Walk through the local antique malls and get an idea of what they carry/accept and what kind of spaces they have to offer. Talk to the owners/managers and get a price sheet for rents/commissions, etc.

MAKE CONNECTIONS – Know the auction houses, art galleries, serious collectors, and long-time dealers in your area. Make sure you network with other non-profits as well. You can refer to each other for item donations that may suit you or them better and generate goodwill from the organization and the donor.

RECYCLING METAL is a great way to raise revenue from things you would normally just toss. Metal is in more things than you think:

Electrical cords

Frames

Kitchen utensils and flatware

Tools

Bathroom and kitchen fixtures

Doorknobs

Computers and other electrical items

Décor items such as metal vases and baskets

Small and large appliances

Toys

Sports equipment

The list goes on. You would be surprised how quickly it can add up. Recruit a volunteer who is willing to train you how to process and prepare the metal for recycling and where to take the metal.

Obtain (by borrowing or purchasing or donation) a trailer for ease of transportation and storage. Use totes to sort the items into by metal type.

Chapter 5

This brings us to the next step: **online sales**.

I would pick 2 – 3 sites to concentrate on or you will have too much to control and accomplish only frustration. Another strategy is to have a team (2-3) doing online sales that ship to a worldwide audience such as Etsy, eBay and Amazon, PLUS someone (1 person is usually enough) handling the local online listings and sales from sites such as Facebook and Craigslist. I have listed these in order of most effective to least effective.

At this point you need to open a PayPal account if you don't already have one. The instructions are easy to follow (You will need proof of your 501(c)(3) status and your Federal Tax ID) and they have the PayPal Giving Fund which removes much of the cost for non-profits. Here is the link to register your non-profit organization and set up an account:

https://www.paypal.com/us/webapps/mpp/donatio ns

Here is a link for the Giving Works program:

https://www.paypal.com/us/webapps/mpp/givingfu nd/home

eBay – FOR EVERYTHING.
https://reg.eBay.com/reg/PartialReg?acntType=bu
siness&_trksid=p2052190.144594

Etsy – FOR COLLECTIBLES, HANDMADE
ITEMS, CRAFT MATERIALS AND THE
UNUSUAL. This is what eBay used to be, and
they are much more customer service friendly
and seller friendly.
https://www.etsy.com/sell?ref=hdr&from_page=ht
tps%3A%2F%2Fwww.etsy.com%2F.

Amazon – FOR BOOKS, ITEMS NEW IN
PACKAGE, ITEMS NEW WITH TAG, CDs,
DVDs, AUDIO BOOKS. If it has an ISBN (books)
or a UPC code (most packaged items under the
bar code), or MPN (manufacturer's Part Number,
many items have this on their sticker or tag if
they have one) then you can list it on Amazon.
You can also search items without those by
typing in the title (media) or what the item is, but
most items will have an MPN on them.
Facebook – FOR EVERYTHING. List your items
on your organization's page, in selling groups for
your area, or general selling groups such as
collectibles or vintage lovers. Nearly every area
(county, state, town) has a selling/trade/barter
group(s). People can be flaky and never show up

to purchase an arranged sale, but it's still free exposer and advertising. You can also have a Facebook store, which is more free exposure for your organization and business (thrift store if you have one). It's free and with $50 or less in Facebook ads, you can build a good following and customer base in fairly short order. https://www.facebook.com/marketplace/

<u>Craigslist</u> – FOR EVERYTHING ESPECIALLY LARGE ITEMS YOU DON'T WANT TO SHIP. Pretty sure we have all heard of this. Online classified ads. Usually by local area, but you can offer shipping to other areas if desired.

<u>Nextdoor</u> – GOOD FOR LARGE ITEMS AND ITEMS OF LOCAL INTEREST. Free advertising! Free private social network for your neighborhood community and surrounding areas. Don't blast your neighbors with posts, but once a week or so will get your organization out there and if you have a thrift store, garner customers and donations. Anything that helps spread the word is worth a few minutes.

<u>Bonanza</u> – FOR EVERYTHING. This site is rising in popularity, but still has a long way to go. Sales may be sparse but you won't be penalized

by listing your items on multiple venues and then deleting them if they sell elsewhere, as you are on EBay. The more exposure for your items the better, but only use this venue if you have plenty of manpower. You can link your Amazon, EBay and Bonanza stores and import to Bonanza.

Pinterest – Have a Pinterest page for your organization. Pinterest is huge. When you list something on one of the above sites, you will be given the opportunity to share the listing on various social media outlets. Share like the wind!

Instagram – Set up an account for your organization. This is photo based, so post appealing and artistic photos (such as grouping items by color or type) to gain attention and followers. In your profile you can have a link to your online sales site, such as Etsy, Facebook, eBay, or your own website.

Another way to sell online are **smartphone Apps**: Listed in order of selling productivity.

Amazon Seller – Use this when doing your initial sort of items. Scan items new in package, new with tags, books, anything with a bar code or ISBN, MPN (manufacturer part number), EIN, etc. Often items will have a sticker, printed number (MPN) or number on the tag such as plush toys. You can look these up as well on Amazon. With a smart phone you can list like the wind with this app while sorting donations, or at least screen them to find the 'good stuff' to separate and list later.

eBay Seller – Pretty much eBay selling on your smart phone. Great for researching possible higher end or collectible items, by searching completed auctions.

Bookscouter – This app checks the lowest price on Amazon while also telling you which online book buyers will purchase the book and for how much. Great way to maximize your media, but use Amazon in conjunction. Sometimes Bookscouter returns a less-than-accurate price for Amazon, so scan a bunch of books (audio books too), and make piles for each seller and a pile for Amazon to list later. If you sell books for paperbacks .50 and hardbacks 1.00, or whatever, then anything over that paid by one of the buyers on the app will be gravy. When you have your piles ready to ship, go online to the buyer's website and register or log in, verify the list of books to sell is correct, then accept and print the shipping label. Yes, they even pay for shipping!

Letgo – For everything. Like Craigslist, it's by location, so it is local (about 60 miles radius) and good advertising if nothing else. Try listing nice things that have sat around for a bit and you can't figure out why. Maybe they need more exposure, like that nice pair of Nike shoes that are an odd size.

Poshmark – For selling clothing, accessories, Home décor, and jewelry. It takes more effort to sell on Poshmark. You can't just list it and forget it. Once you learn the ins and outs of Poshmark selling, though, it can be quite lucrative. There are lots of great YouTube videos on Poshmark selling and I also recommend this book: *Poshmark Unlocked: Unlock the strategies and techniques to create a 6-figure income on Poshmark!* by Shannon Jean

Mercari – For selling everything. This is a very popular and profitable selling site/platform/app and easy to use.

Decluttr – They buy CDs. DVDs, games, and tech. They don't pay a whole lot, so I use this when I'm about to half price something or pull it because it hasn't sold. Something is better than nothing.

Threadflip – Some sellers make good money on this app, selling brand name and designer clothing.

Sites you should visit to learn from and stay in touch with the resale and thrift world:

Thriftflipper.com
Thriftaway.wordpress.com
Thriftstoreflipping.com
Yardsalequeen.com
YouTube.com

Now you'll want to know **how to maximize your sales online and minimize your expenses.** Lots of guides explain selling on Etsy, eBay, Amazon, etc. but here is a nimble strategy for being a top online seller.

Minimum needed for online sales:
- Volunteer(s) to sort, research, photograph and list online items
- Office (donated space or part of space already rented/owned)
- Internet service (fast and reliable) Compare local providers, ask about 501c3 discounts
- Computer (Ask on Facebook free and buy nothing groups)
- Shelving (Again, ask for donations of shelving)
- 2 tables 4-6' each – 1 for photography, 1 for packing orders
- White sheet or table cloth (for photo background)
- Packing materials – boxes, bubble wrap, popcorn, tape (ask for donations of these!)
- Printer (Facebook again!)
- Paper for printer

- Ink for printer (eBay is the cheapest for printer ink)
- Your volunteers can use their smart phones to take pictures, or you can invest in a good digital camera or hope one gets donated, or even buy one from a non-profit thrift store. Support each other!

Another great resource for advertising and donations:
https://nextdoor.com/find-neighborhood/

Time is money. You don't want to waste time looking for your ordered items. It's important to have an inventory storage system. Keep it simple. Have a room (or part of a large room) lined with shelves like a library, against the walls and down the center to make isles. Start with 1A and label each shelf on the first section. The next section (shelving unit) start with B1, and so on until you run out of shelves. On eBay, you can put the shelf location of the item in the Custom Label (SKU) space and it will come up on the order when it is sold, so you won't have to search.

I will only cover the 3 major sellers: Amazon, eBay and Etsy. With much experimentation I have found they are really the ones to concentrate on as a seller.

<u>EBAY</u>: Non-profit sellers on eBay can join the eBay for Charity which has partnered with the PayPal Giving Fund to make it easy for sellers to donate some or all of the proceeds from eBay listings to their favorite charities.

Sellers have two options when listing items to benefit charities on eBay:

Community Selling: Donate up to 100% of your final sales price to support your chosen charities. You can customize the donation percentage and the charity you want to support for each individual listing (save it to a template to save time!). The minimum donation amount is 10% or $1, or 1% for eBay Motors listings.

Direct Selling: You can associate an eBay username with a specific charity. All sales associated with this username are considered Direct Selling for the charity, and 100% of selling proceeds will benefit that named nonprofit.

When you choose to donate to a charity, as a charity you want to choose the 100% option and the non-profit organization it goes to, being your organization.

However, if you know regular donors who sell on eBay, make them aware of the option to donate a percentage of their sales to your organization. Hey, can't hurt!

Once you register as a non-profit, choose to have 100% of your proceeds benefit your organization. If others are selling and donating to your organization, three weeks after the sale, PayPal Giving Fund will automatically collect the donation from any sellers donating to your non-profit. Here's how it works:

When you or other sellers designate a charity, the organization's logo and description will appear in the listing description, and eBay notifies the charity that the listing has been created. (The organization can request to have the listing canceled if they prefer not to be associated with the listing.) So each listing is free advertising for your organization!

You, as a <u>seller</u>, will pay standard insertion and final value fees for your listings. However, when your item sells, you'll receive a refund for the insertion fee and the final value fee. BUT if your item does not sell, and the listing expires, you still have to pay the insertion fee.

In other words:

You list the item and pay an insertion fee.
Your item does not sell.
You relist the item and pay another insertion fee.
Your item sells this time.
The second insertion fee plus the final value fee
are both refunded.

The key to maximizing here is:

Utilize your free listings. Each seller, depending
on how long they have been selling and their
seller standing, gets a certain number of free
listings a month. It's pretty low to start out,
about 20 free listings, so you will have to pay
listing fees to build your seller standing if you
want to speed up the process of 'leveling up' to get
more free listings per month. If you only have a
few items to list in the beginning, then stop when
you reach your free listing limit, or chose to pay
.35 a listing.

However, if you have a lot to list, remember that
if the item sells within the first listing period
(about a month for buy-it-now listing or 3-10 days
as you chose for auction listings) then you pay
NO FEES. To accomplish this, research what

same/similar items have sold for (if they haven't sold, then don't list yours) and match or beat the lowest price for a like item in the same condition as yours. About 10 days or a week from the time your items are set to expire, if they haven't sold, put a Make Offer option on all of them, allowing buyers to bargain. You can also discount the price by amount or percentage to help them move out the door. If your item is on auction, let it finish unchanged. Many buyers wait until the last second to bid!

How to choose between a Buy-It-Now listing or an auction listing: When researching your items, if you find no similar items, or your item is in much better condition than the items that have sold, or if only a couple of similar items have sold and brought decent prices, list your item as an auction, and let the market decide it's value. Start your opening price at the minimum you want to get for the item. If you find a lot of items similar to the one you are researching, and a majority of them have sold, price yours at the lowest price achieved and list it as a Buy-It-Now. Check the current listings as well as the completed listings. Make sure you are not pricing above what is currently for sale.

If you are selling a larger number of items, say more than 50 a month, then you want to consider opening an eBay store. You get additional free listings with the cost of the store, which should save you fees if listing a larger number of items because the store fee will be less than all those listing fees added up. Then you won't be so pressured to sell an item the first time around, thus simplifying the process for you. Also, a store allows you to showcase your organization with a banner, your logo, an introduction blurb about your organization and mission, etc.

If all goes well according to the above, you will be paying a minimum of fees with a maximum of sales.

Once a month, reevaluate your listings and tweak titles, descriptions, and shipping. Did you list it at priority when it can go first class? Items that have not sold after 3 times around should not remain online but be displayed in your store, UNLESS it's an expensive item that may take a while to sell, and be worth it when it does.

If you have a thrift store or other 'brinks and mortar' venue for items, have a floor for your eBay items. That is, don't list an item priced at or below what you think you can get in person. Try them in your store first, and if the item doesn't sell in person, then list it online. You want to offer nice things in your store and online. With experimentation and experience you will find a price point at which things don't sell in the store when they go above that price (for the most part) depending on your location and clientele. For most of the stores I have managed, that price is $20, with certain exceptions. For example, if you are an animal rescue organization, and you get a brand new or like pet crate or large cage or other higher-priced item donated (Amazon sells it for $100, for instance) then you can ask $50 or so, and save yourself the trouble of shipping it. These would be good items to advertise on Facebook or Craigslist.

Here is an example done for a mid-level non-profit seller on eBay:

Without the store, they received 50 free listings per month (after selling online for one year and building their account) and paid $0.35 per listing for items that didn't sell, which was about 300 listings. Fifty of those were free, leaving them with about 250 listings that didn't sell. Multiply those by $.35 and you get $87.50.

They set up an online store (which has a bunch of benefits beyond getting more free listings). Using the approximately 250 unsold listings last month, they went with the second level store which costs $21.95 per month (with an annual commitment) and comes with 250 free listings per month (it actually comes with 250 fixed price listings and 250 auction listings, but they mostly use fixed price listings) and $0.25 per listing after that. So, as an example, if they had done this before last month's bill, they would have had 300 unsold listings, 250 of which would have been free. That would have left 50 listings at $0.25 for a total of $12.50. Add that to the $21.95 monthly fee for the store and their bill would have been about $34.45, saving about 53.05.

eBay also has Seller Hub which is a nifty platform giving you oodles of analytics and marketing assistance. There is also an active forum which has great interaction and info. eBay also has 2 YouTube channels: eBay and Selling on eBay which are very helpful.

eBay also has a batch edit feature which is super convenient and time saving. You can mark prices up, down, add Make Offer button, etc.

When researching and listing, price your item at or just below the lowest comparable that has sold or is currently listed. You can sort the results of a search by newly listed, ending soonest, or price low to high or vice versa. Sort by lowest to highest and then match or beat that price for the same item you have in the same condition. After 3 weeks, and add Make Offer to the listings, hopefully giving the items a push out the door by accepting reasonable offers before the listings end and you have to pay for another 30 days.

A significant portion of sales these days are via mobile devices, so check your listings every so often to make sure they are attractive on mobile devices. For more information go to:

https://pages.eBay.com/sell/itemdescription/mobil efriendlyguidelines.html

New items go to the top of searches, so list your items for the '30 days, not good until cancelled' option. Then when they expire, sort them by price high to low, and renew the higher-priced items first, using your free listings. Mark the price down 10% or so to entice sales. Or add a Make an Offer button so customers can haggle. Remember, each time your item doesn't sell in a 30 day listing, you must pay another listing fee, until it sells and that last listing fee is refunded. So if you list it once and it sells within the first 30 days, it's completely free. You can do this easily with MARKDOWN MANAGER.

When you list items in your store, you put them in categories, such as books, jewelry, clothes, etc. A useful tactic is to have a sale on a category a month, marking those items down by dollar amount or percentage. Again, Markdown Manager can help you breeze through this.

Keep an eye out for free listing days! eBay has them occasionally, and it's great to take advantage of them. They are advertised beforehand, so you can plan your staffing around listing as much as possible those free listing days.

When there is a free listings special for auctions, pick the items you think will have the best chance of selling OR listings that have been on a long time and you want to move out the door. Start the auction a few dollars less than the BIN (buy it now) you previously had the item listed for. Then include an appropriate BIN, say just under the previous BIN the item was listed for. What is the least you would sell the item for? Start the auction there. If the item goes too low in price, pull it and sell it in your store or at a rummage sale, etc.

When listing your items, make sure you chose the best listing type for the item: auction (items you can't find info on or don't know enough about to research properly), fixed price (items you find plenty of info on and can price according to recent sales).

Sell internationally through eBay's Global Shipping Program. It's just like shipping domestically, and will increase your sales.

Skip listing upgrades such as highlight and bold for your titles. They only put money into the coffers of eBay.

Offer combined shipping discounts to encourage customers to purchase more than one item. You can also offer multiple purchases discounts for customers purchasing more than one item. I would choose one or the other, not both, or you will be short selling yourself with the combined discounts. You can set both of these up as you list each item, or in edit or batch edit on your current listings.

When setting up your store or seller page, fill out the FAQ for customers to save everyone time.

They may also help someone feel more confident in you as a seller and result in more sales.

List seasonal items at least 2 months prior to the holiday or season.

Jan-Feb: Valentines

March-April: St. Patrick's, spring fashion, golf, baseball.

July-Aug: Camping, hunting, fishing, back to school, golf.

Sept-Oct: Winter fashions, coats and outerwear, boots, skiing, Halloween, fall/harvest, football.

Nov-Dec: Christmas, Thanksgiving.

ETSY: There is currently no program for non-profits on Etsy, however, there are some ways to boost sales worth knowing about. Go to your shop manager > Seller Handbook. Forums are also very helpful.

Etsy is a great place for vintage clothing, décor, craft, and unique items. While I recommend listing items on multiple channels, such as collectible books on Amazon and Etsy and eBay, or new items on eBay and Amazon, there are some things to take care with. Inventory is important, so make sure to remove an item from all venues when it sells. Also, eBay is very strict about ending listings early, and will penalize you if you sell items on another venue then cancel the listing on eBay or cancel too many sales if you happen to get two orders for the same item. Just stay on top of it and be careful. Etsy is a great marketplace for collectibles and vintage items. It is superior in many ways to eBay.

- The prices realized are often higher.
- shoppers are more courteous and more reliable overall.
- Etsy advertises more and has holiday promotions that eBay does not.
- They have a great Seller Handbook that encompasses hundreds of articles and an active forum.
- Etsy has a marketing menu on your Shop Manager menu. This includes easy ways to market on social media, such as sharing listings or a link to your store on Facebook, Twitter, Instagram and Pinterest.
- You can also easily make coupons and run sales, which do make a difference.
- Etsy doesn't care if you list items on other venues and will not penalize you for it, so

you can also sell on Facebook, Bonanza, Google, etc.

- Etsy has 2 YouTube Channels! Etsy and Etsy Success. They are both very helpful.

On eBay listings are .35; on Etsy, they are .20, but there are no free listings on Etsy. eBay listings are for 30 days where Etsy listings are good for 4 months! So, you have more time to work your listings. After it's been up a month, re-evaluate your listing. Add new search words, tweak your title, make sure all the attributes are filled in, etc. Make sure your shipping is accurate or offer free shipping on small items that will be inexpensive to ship. This way you can move more items without having to pay the .20 per item renewal fee.

When setting up your Etsy shop, make sure everything is filled out such as shop policies and the About You section, have a unique banner or logo, set your processing/handling times to the lowest possible (people like instant gratification and quick shipping), set shipping profiles to save time on listing, etc. Read articles in the Sellers Handbook. They are quick and easy to follow and really help. Study your analytics to see where traffic is coming from and for clues on how to increase sales (conversion rate).

AMAZON:

First, you must register for a seller account. Go to this page

You will need you organization's banking info, a contact name/person for the account, and their ID to prove they are a real person and not someone trying to set up a fraudulent account. Your organization's Executive Director or bookkeeper/treasurer/financial Director, might be a good choice to set up the account, or you will be texting, scanning and phoning a lot.

Once your account is set up and activated (you will get notified by Amazon), you can start listing!

There are some items that are restricted on Amazon, such as some DVDs, CDs, and certain electrical items, that can only be sold by 'approved sellers.' For those items, just list them on eBay for the same price you would list it for on Amazon. Amazon, just like eBay and Etsy, have a list of items you cannot sell on their site. Make sure to review these restrictions so you don't break any rules and raise red flags on your account. You can find all the pertinent information on your Amazon Seller Central page at the top right under Help – Policies and Agreements.

<u>Prohibited or Restricted Products</u>:

Alcohol
Animals & Animal-Related Products
Art - Fine Art
Art - Home Decor
Automotive and Powersports
Composite Wood Products
Cosmetics & Skin/Hair Care
Currency, Coins, Cash Equivalents, and Gift Cards
Dietary Supplements
Drugs & drug paraphernalia
Electronics
Explosives, Weapons, and Related Items
Export Controls
Food & Beverage
Gambling & Lottery
Hazardous and Dangerous Items
Human Parts & Burial Artifacts
Jewelry & Precious Gems
Laser products
Lighting
Lock Picking & Theft Devices

Medical devices and accessories
Offensive and Controversial Materials
Pesticides and Pesticide Devices
Plants, Plant Products, and Seeds
Postage Meters & Stamps
Recalled Products
Recycling electronics
Sex & Sensuality
Subscriptions and Periodicals
Surveillance Equipment
Tobacco & Tobacco-Related Products
Warranties, Service Plans, Contracts, and Guarantees
Other Restricted Products

In order to maintain a good seller status, ship items within one business day of the order being placed. Include a packing slip as a courtesy to your customer, unless they request otherwise. You can print the packing slip and shipping label from your orders screen.

Chapter 7

SHIPPING – It is easy to lose money on shipping if you don't list weight and dimensions properly, or chose the correct shipping service. For instance, items over 3 pounds go cheaper via FedEx Saver delivery than USPS Priority. Listing your item with both choices can help you sell the item, because expensive shipping can stop a customer from buying your item.

You will be having regular shipments (hopefully) so call your local post office and arrange for regular postal service, delivery and pick up, if you don't already have it.

PACKING YOUR ITEM(S)

You want secure items but not overdone and thus wasting supplies. All parts need to be wrapped individually. Even electronics and chargers, etc.

Make sure there is 1-3" on all sides depending on fragility of the item. You want the item wrapped in bubble wrap or foam, then nested in popcorn or wadded plastic bags. Paper weighs more and I personally hate the ink on newspapers.

Tape the box securely! A couple strips along the seams and then a cross piece like + on top and bottom. I've only had a couple packages pop open during shipment, but it's a real bummer when they do.

NOTE: Evaluate the item before you list it. Will it need insurance? Extra packaging such as for dish sets or fragile items? Make sure to add that in or you will have a loss on shipping.

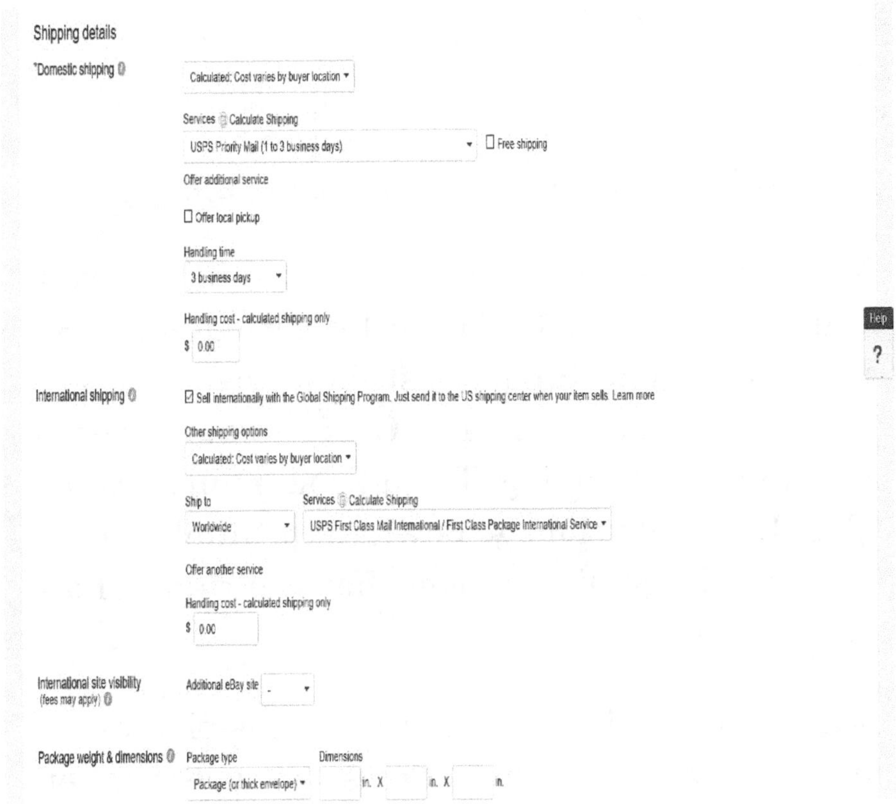

Shipping details

*Domestic shipping ⓘ

Calculated: Cost varies by buyer location ▾

Services ⓘ Calculate Shipping

USPS Priority Mail (1 to 3 business days) ▾ ☐ Free shipping

Offer additional service

☐ Offer local pickup

Handling time

3 business days ▾

Handling cost - calculated shipping only

$ 0.00

International shipping ⓘ

☑ Sell internationally with the Global Shipping Program. Just send it to the US shipping center when your item sells. Learn more

Other shipping options

Calculated: Cost varies by buyer location ▾

Ship to | Services ⓘ Calculate Shipping

Worldwide ▾ | USPS First Class Mail International / First Class Package International Service ▾

Offer another service

Handling cost - calculated shipping only

$ 0.00

International site visibility
(fees may apply) ⓘ

Additional eBay site - ▾

Package weight & dimensions ⓘ Package type | Dimensions

Package (or thick envelope) ▾ | in. X ___ in. X ___ in.

Help

?

EBay Shipping page

Etsy shipping page with profiles set up.

You can set up as many shipping profiles as you want. I do profiles for USPS Priority (items 1-3 pounds), FedEx Smart Post (items over 3 pounds), media mail, First Class (items under 15 oz), and free shipping. To add a shipping profile click Duplicate then go down to the duplicated one and click Edit, change what you want, and save.

NOTE: Items that have large dimensions can have an oversized surcharge, so be sure to enter your package dimensions as you estimate them to be when the item is packaged. To estimate the size of the item with packaging, add 2" to each side of the item.

Choose the CALCULATED SHIPPING. It's so much easier.

For added sales, offer combined shipping. That means the customer pays the regular price for the first item shipped and an additional amount you enter for each added item. For both eBay and Etsy, you can put in pre-saved shipping profiles for multiple classes of mail and there is a box to enter a price for 'additional items' if they purchase more than one thing from you.

Weigh each item. Smaller items like jewelry, small toys, small figurines, or ornaments that weigh 10 ounces or less can go first class. Just put in 15 ounces as their weight and you should be good for packaging. The point is to be a bit under to make some to cover the cost of shipping supplies. Get as much donated as you can, such as bubble wrap, popcorn, boxes, bubble envelopes, etc. But there are always things you'll need to buy, like tape, printing paper, etc.

If the item is over or close to a pound, add one pound for packaging, unless it is books which can go media mail. If it's a heavier item that is not breakable and does not need a lot of packaging, then add 10 ounces. Large plush animals, shoes, coats, etc. can usually go into padded or poly envelopes or boxes without packing. If it is a multi-piece item, such as dishes, cups, and saucers, etc., then add 1.5-2 pounds for packaging. You want them to get there intact, so pack well, but don't over pack and waste materials. Make sure your item has at least 1-2" on each side of

packing material/padding, and is snug but not tight in the package. Plastic bags wadded up and packed around an item is a cheap and secure way to send items, especially if you get a lot of bags donated, which you will if you ask. Use a layer of bubble wrap around the item, just to make sure. The idea is to nest the item in a secure cocoon of wadded plastic bags and bubble wrap. The wrapped item should not be in contact with any of the sides, top, or bottom of the box.

Lastly, make sure your dimensions are correct or close. Add about 2 inches to each side of the item when entering dimensions for shipping. If the item is larger, the dimensions packaged could kick it into oversized surcharge, costing you quite a bit, so measure and enter with packaging in mind. Don't be hesitant to cut a box down to fit your needs. Always remember, though, you want to make a good impression, so use clean, good-looking packing and shipping materials.

For items $100 and over, I would require
signature delivery. There are a lot of porch
pirates out there right now. It will cost a
bit extra, but it's worth it. Tracking is included
free of charge on all packages, EXCEPT some
international shipments. Before you purchase the
shipping label, make sure the free tracking is
noted. You may not want to ship to countries that
tracking is not available for. You can choose US
shipping only, or handpick the countries you will
ship to, or choose worldwide and ship
everywhere.

Note at very bottom of the listing form where you
can choose countries to exclude for shipping.

When actually shipping the item, after it's packed
and on the scale, enter the actual dimensions and
weight and then explore the pull down options for
flat rate priority, regular priority, UPS ground,

Fed Ex Home Delivery, USPS ground, especially for large and/or heavy items. Reiterating what I said earlier about choosing the right delivery method, this will make sure you are getting the best postage deal.

Shipping Classes USPS:

Media Mail

- CDs, DVDs, books, & educational materials.
- No advertising, so magazines and catalogs are a no-no.
- It's slow, 3-8 business days, but it's cheap. If it's going to Alaska or Hawaii, it can take up to 3 weeks.

First Class

- Items 15oz or less when packaged.
- 1-3 days delivery
- Needs to be at least ½" thick to have tracking

Priority Mail

- Items over 1lb when packaged.
- 1-3 days delivery
- Tracking is included.
- USPS provides free shipping materials for Priority Mail

Standard Post (ground)

- 2-8 business days delivery
- Can be good for oversized packages
- Often the price is almost the same as Priority

Express Mail

- Next day delivery
- Good for Christmas and birthdays or urgently needed items
- Expensive but good to offer it and the buyer will pay if they need it.

For more info visit https://www.usps.com/ship/mail-shipping-services.htm

For Priority Mail free supplies: https://store.usps.com/store/home

But-- Don't buy other shipping materials here; you can get them cheaper at Wal-Mart, uline.com, or eBay.

What you need to have on hand:

- Packing peanuts (some hate these and refuse to use them, but I hate newspaper. I find it weighs the least and protects the best. However, used plastic bags wadded up to form a nice thick cushion on all sides works great too and you can get those donated by the trunk full.

- Padded bubble envelopes/mailers
- Photo mailer (ridged)
- Tape (Shipping not scotch or masking tape)
- Boxes of various sizes and priority boxes
- Bubble wrap
- Box cutter
- Scissors
- Shipping digital scale (you can get these at the USPS where they cost a bit more, or on Amazon or eBay where they cost a bit less.)
- Printer – Thermal or Laser for printing packing slips and shipping labels.
- Printer paper
- Computer

If something does go awry in your shipping an order, handle the issue promptly and with courteous customer service. Golden rule!

You can file missing mail inquiries (make sure all items have a tracking number) and claims for broken items (make sure you insure for enough) from the usps.com site.

Ship only one item at a time, so you won't get orders mixed up and send the wrong person the wrong item.

Also, it's a great idea to offer local pick up of the item, so local customers can purchase with ease and not have to contact you about getting a special invoice without shipping.

Here is where you choose the OFFER LOCAL PICKUP option on your item listing form:

Shipping details

'Domestic shipping ⓘ   Calculated: Cost varies by buyer location ▾

Services ☷ Calculate Shipping

FedEx SmartPost (2 to 8 business days)   ▾   ☐ Free shipping

Offer additional service

☐ Offer local pickup

Handling time

3 business days   ▾

Handling cost - calculated shipping only

$ 0.00

AMAZON: This is a great venue for:

- New items: that is, items in a sealed package or with tags still attached
- Media such as books, DVDs, CDs, games (electronic and otherwise)

The keys to successful listings are much the same as eBay and Etsy: good description and photos.

Most regular items have photos already, but if you list collectible or unusual items, include photos in your listing. Many sellers have minimal descriptions on Amazon, so go a step further and put a sentence or three about your item and customers will be more likely to buy yours over your close competitors just because they are clearer about what they are getting.

Shipping on Amazon can be tricky, as they assign the amounts you get compensated. Also, in order to be competitive, you must often offer free shipping. For small, light items, this is not so much of an issue. However, as you get into board games and heavier electronics, profit can get sticky.

Look up the item in the search bar. Click the listing that matches. Click on the for sale listings that match your item (used, hardback, paperback, new, etc.) and note that Amazon sorts them least to most expensive. You need to be in the top 3 to be competitive. The ones with free shipping come up first, SO you need to factor price to get into the top three.

Example: I'm selling a card game. It is small and will ship for about $3.50. The top two sellers are offering theirs at $19.00 with free shipping. So I go to list my item and see Amazon will give me $4.99 in shipping credit. Thus I price mine at $14.00, meaning the item will be at $18.99 total, thus in the top spot and most visible to buyers.

BUT, if your game weights over 1 pound, then it will have to go priority mail, and that starts at about $8.00. In that case I would need to weigh the item and estimate how much packing would weigh and how much it would cost to send to a state on the other side of the US from you just to be safe. The average is about $11.00. Now your item still lists for $14.00, but with the extra postage will realize $7.99. Amazon also charges $1.00 to list your item plus a percentage of the total sale including shipping. This is what your fees would look like:

Std Dom Ship $4.99   Fees $3.84   Net $15.15

But then you must take out the shipping cost (which you buy through Amazon at a discount)

The item weighed 1.8 pounds packaged, so shipping would be $11-12.00 depending on destination. If it could fit in a small priority flat rate box it would be about $7.00 with your Amazon discount.

$15.15 - \$12 = \$3.15$ Net (regular priority shipping)

$15.15 - \$7 = \$8.15$ Net (small flat rate priority shipping)

$15.15 - \$2.70 = \$12.45$ (approximate first class shipping items under 15oz)

SO this is where you need to take some time and evaluate if the item is online worthy, Amazon worthy, or just fit for sale in your store or rummage sale. If you only sell online, $3.15 is better than $1.00 at a rummage sale or nothing. Yet, It may sell just as well on eBay or Etsy for a better return.

Once you do this for a bit, you'll get good at eye-balling numbers, sizes, and weights and know pretty quickly what's worth it and what's not.

MONEY MAKING TIP:

Items 15oz or under: $5.00 minimum listing price.

Items that can go media mail (books, CDs, DVDs, records, cassettes): $5.00 minimum listing price. Much like first class but up to 3 pounds due to reduced media mail prices.

Items over 1 pound: $12-14 minimum listing price depending on size and weight.

For $40 a month, you can have a pro seller account on Amazon.

Benefits of a Professional Selling Plan

- No $0.99 Closing Fee for each item sold. You pay only a monthly $39.99 subscription fee, referral fees, and variable closing fees
- Ability to collect U.S. sales and use taxes on your orders
- Customize your shipping rates and services levels for all products (except Books, Music, Videos and DVDs)
- Manage your inventory using feeds, spreadsheets, and reports
- Manage orders using order reports and order-related feeds
- Access Amazon Marketplace Web Service to upload feeds, receive reports, and perform other API functions
- Ability to offer Promotions and Gift Services
- Eligibility for Featured Merchant status and listing placement in the Buy Box

You must provide business info and other documentation to be a Pro Seller. And this option is only worth it if you list more than 50 items a month.

You can also have Amazon ship your orders with Fulfillment By Amazon, but you must pay them to store your items and you must ship them to Amazon to store in the first place, so I really see no gain in that unless you deal in large volume. There are plenty of articles and discussions on FBA online, so read a few and judge for yourself.

Here are the details of FBA from Amazon themselves:

The videos on Seller Central are invaluable. They are short and easy. Start at the top and go down the list, watching items pertinent to where you are as a seller. The link is below to get you started:

https://sellercentral.amazon.com/learn/ref=xx_su_foot_home

Shipping supplies and where to get them!

Get as many used items as possible donated, such as reusable boxes, bubble wrap, packing popcorn, etc. Sometimes, however, you need outstrips the supply, so here are links to the cost-effective supplies I purchase:

MONEY SAVE TIP! If your organization has Amazon Prime, great! If not, then have a volunteer or employee who does have Amazon Prime purchase the items with free shipping and reimburse them.

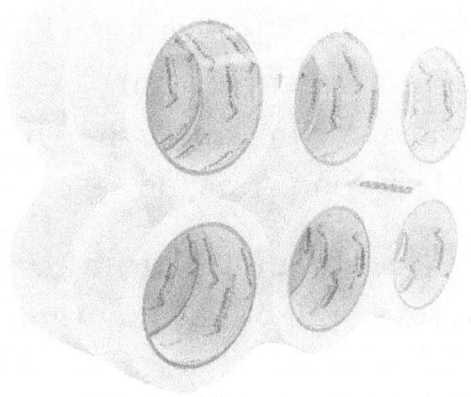

For bubble mailer envelopes, I usually get boxes of 100 size #5 which is 10.5x15". This size will fit nearly everything, or can be cut down or you can use 2 envelopes for really large items. This is the most cost effective way I have found. EBay is the cheapest for these. My favorite seller is Supply Hut, but don't be afraid to compare prices with others. Prices on eBay fluctuate daily, just like the stock market.

From the above seller I get bubble wrap, packing popcorn and bubble mailers cheaper than anywhere else. Right now, for instance, they have packing tape for even less than Amazon.

Polly mailers are great for shipping clothing, fabric, bedding, plush toys, and other like items.

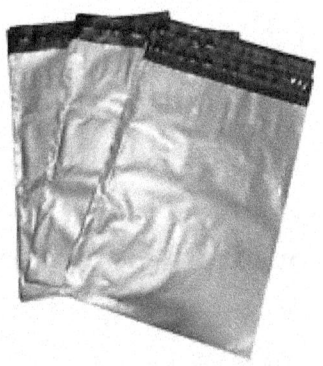

MONEY SAVING TIP: For packing instead of using peanuts, use wadded plastic bags. They work great and everyone has bunches they want to get rid of. Don't use paper; it weighs more than popcorn or plastic bags and you want to save every half an ounce possible.

Here are my two favorite shipping scales:

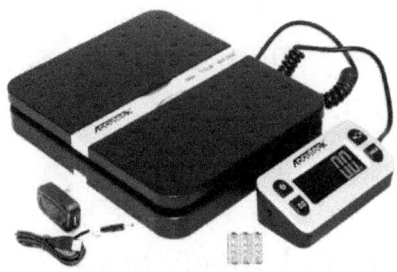

Trust me, you want one of these:

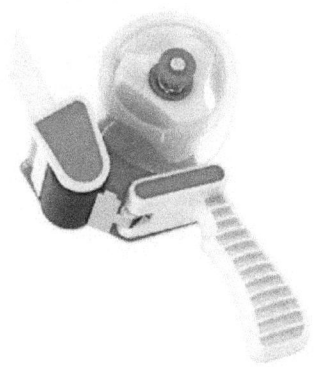

Makes life so much easier.

Chapter 8

How to make a listing that will convert into sales:
This section is applicable for every selling venue.

The title is the essential hook to get a customer to click on your item. It is also essential in getting higher rankings in search results. So write a clear title with these essentials:

- Brand, signature, origin
- Color
- Size – clothing
- If clothing or accessories – men's, women's, children's, or non-gender
- Material(s)
- Age, style or era
- Graham weight for gold and silver items

Make sure everything is spelled correctly. Avoid using adjectives such as amazing, very nice, look, wow, etc. Don't abbreviate except for commonly used terms such as:

NWT (New with Tag)

NIB (New in Box)

NIP (New in Package)

NOS (New Old Stock) Items discovered in warehouses or closed stores that were never sold and are still as new.

FS (Factory Sealed)

Photographs are essential in selling items online. They should be against a white or neutral background that shows the item clearly. The lighting should be good but not overly bright as to wash out the colors and details. Beware of flash or glare reflecting off of shiny objects. Photograph from every angle: front, back, sides, and bottom. Show close-ups of marks or tags or signatures. Provide detailed pictures of any damage, flaws, pattern, or special feature that may add value to the item.

You can use a digital camera or a smartphone, but cameras will give the best pictures.

The description will often make the difference between a customer thinking about it or buying it. Descriptions should be clear, cover all major issues or attributes, the style or pattern, the materials the item is made of, and any bonus info you think might help, such as 'I only used this twice,' or 'looks unused and works like a charm.' If you need keywords, vital for your item to show up in the top results of searches, use Google Ad

Words or look up similar listings and see what words they used.

Offering free shipping on small items or light non-breakable items can make a big difference.

On Amazon, if you don't find the item you have, go to your Seller Central > Inventory > Add a Product. Then enter the title (if it's a book) or the name of the product. Enter the ISBN or UPC. Select a category. Make sure to fill in as much as possible under the Vital Info tab. Under the Offer Tab enter the price, SKU, the number of items you have of that particular product, condition (be thorough, Amazon buyers are vocal), and shipping options offered. On the Images tab, make sure to include a picture, unless there is already a stock photo that exactly matches yours.

Selling DVDs and CDs priced over $25 is restricted on Amazon, so the best venue for those is eBay.

Key shopping dates:

June – Sept

Wedding Season

Biggest sales for sellers specializing in wedding items are usually seen in June and July. Think jewelry, formal clothing, crystal stemware, punch sets, table cloths, linen napkins, china sets. This is an excellent time to move otherwise stagnant china sets. It is cheaper than renting china, and currently it is popular to have mix-and-match vintage china at your wedding.

<u>Sept</u>

Labor Day Sales

Many sellers and retailers run Labor Day sales to get rid of excess inventory accrued during the busy summer donation season.

<u>July – Aug</u>

Back to School

Dorm or apartment décor, fashion, bags, sell for students gearing up to go away to college. Items that sell during this time are lamps, twin sheet sets and blankets, organizing items, especially for the closet and desk, laundry baskets/hampers. Etc.

This is an excellent time to put out backpacks, and book bags.

<u>Sept - Oct</u>

Halloween

Goth, spooky, autumn, harvest, fall decor, costume supplies and accessories.

<u>Oct – Dec 20</u>

Christmas gift shopping

Get as much as possible listed online by mid-October and keep listing steadily until about Dec 15.

Make sure to put out clean, complete, and working toys. Get batteries at the dollar store and include them with the battery operated toys and Christmas décor. You can mark the price up a dollar or two as a result and they fly off the shelves.

<u>Dec 25- early January</u>

Christmas gift spenders

Lure in people who received money or gift cards as gifts with sales and specials.

Chapter 9

What donations do we REALLY want to maximize?

Sell everything you can at reasonable, even cheap prices. BUT if it's worth $50 don't sell it for .50. If it's worth $10 don't sell it for .25, etcetera. So how do you find the stuff worth more effort and attention?

For instance, Legos bring good money, even loose ones. Collect loose ones until you fill a baggie (sandwich size) and price at $5 a baggie. Look up sets online. Individual mini figures go for $3 and up online, so look those up.

Hallmark ornaments in boxes, Old World Christmas ornaments and other name brand holiday décor should bring $3-10 each. Sometimes more, so look them up.

Power tools and chargers for such in good condition are desirable, so look those up online before putting them in a rummage sale or your thrift store.

In a nutshell, anything pre-1990 needs further attention and research.

Another rule of thumb is if you say "I remember that from my childhood' or 'my gramma had one of those' and you are at least 40, then chances are it might be collectible.

Essential websites for the dealer and collector:

www.kovels.com - a lot of great stuff is free, but their Premium Plus Subscription for $59.99 per year is worth it for accessing their massive database of Maker marks and patterns. However, you can still access a huge amount of info without a paid subscription.

https://www.collectorsweekly.com – A wealth of information about collectibles, collecting, and selling.

https://www.liveauctioneers.com – Fun site where you can watch live auctions and find nearby auction houses. Great for educational purposes. Proxybid.com is another site.

https://www.antiquetrader.com/ - Great info and articles about everything antique or collectible.

https://www.collect.com/ - A page that is access to a variety of specialty collector pages. Hours of entertainment and education.

www.antiqueweek.com – another varied and vast resource

An invaluable site for flatware and china:

https://www.replacements.com

https://www.replacements.com/sell-to-us/

The key to marketing any item is identify it first. Once you get an idea of what you have, check eBay and Etsy for similar items in current listings and ended listings. List your item at a reasonable price based on similar sold and for sale items. If you can't determine a value for your item, do an auction, starting the item at a reasonable price. I usually start around $10-20 depending on availability, condition, visual appeal, and let 'er rip. Make the title attention-getting with lots of keywords, dates, etc. to draw in the bidders.

How to research prices on eBay:

1) 1) Searching: In the search field type in what you have. If the item has a mark or name type that in. If you can identify the style or era of the item then put that in, such as 'mid-century tin spoon with wood handle.' Put as many keywords in as possible. If one combination doesn't work, such as 'pottery blue pitcher' try 'pottery pitcher blue holly design studio made.'

2) 2) Results from your search will come up in current auctions first, that is auctions currently running. Check those to see if there are items like yours and what sellers are asking for them. Next, on the left-hand side of the screen check the box for COMPLETED AUCTIONS and check for your item there. Scrutinize how much they sold for or if they even sold.

3) 3) Pricing: If there are a lot of items listed like your item, then how many are selling versus not selling? (Sold listings are in green price while unsold listings are in black price.) At the top of the results on the right-hand side there is a SORT BY drop; choose lowest to highest. Look at the lowest an item just like yours sold for. Match that price. If there are many currently listed, start or offer your item just below what the lowest asking price is currently for an item just like yours in the same condition.

4) 4)   What if there are no results for an item you're looking for? Or what if I can't identify the item enough to search for it? Check Google under the SHOPPING tab. Check Etsy (Only current items listed are available for searching.) Still nothing? Auction time! Start the item at the price you or a competitor might sell it for in your/their store. Do a 5-7 day auction, timing it to end on a Saturday or Sunday.

5) 5)   If you find the item and it's not selling online well, or it is selling for what you would ask for it in your store/sale/etc. Then just price it and put it out, saving you time and effort photographing, listing, packing, etc.

6) Etsy doesn't have ended (purchased) items, but you can see what is currently being offered and get a fuller picture of the selling market in addition to EBay.

Keys to a good eBay/Etsy/online listing:

1) Clean the item if it's dusty or dirty. (Baby wipes are great for this!)

2) Clear photos against a white or black background, depending on the item's color or finish.

3) Good lighting.

4) Photograph all aspects of the item from front, rear, bottom, etc.
5) Photograph any flaws or damage to the item.
6) The title should be coherently written with as many keywords as possible. Include style, era, color, pattern, marks, etc. in the title. Anything you think someone might search for)
7) The description should be clear and include all points of interest such as measurements, flaws, damage, marks, etc. Do this even if you repeat your title in the description, because the title and description are often searched separately by the database.
8) Make sure shipping weight and measurements are accurate. Imagine the item packaged. Add at least a pound for glass and fragile items, and 2 inches on each side for packing. Choose the calculated shipping for most items.
9) When shipping the item out, pack well. Do not over pack, but make sure the item is snug in the box with at least 1" (2" is better) of padding on each side. Ask for donations of used popcorn, padded mailers, boxes, bubble wrap, and other shipping supplies.

TRUTH: The Four Values of Collectibles:

- The price the owner of the item thinks it is worth.
- The price the buyer of the item would like to pay.
- The price listed in a Price Guide.
- The actual price realized when it sells to a private buyer, a dealer, online such as eBay, or at an auction.

Chapter 10

By now you should have a steady stream of donations and a small team of volunteers sorting and marketing them. You should already have a computer and printer and packing/shipping supplies if you have been selling online.

What if you have a large river of donations and not just a stream? What if your storage isn't enough and you're thinking of having a rummage sale every month?

Perhaps it's time to consider opening a thrift store or bargain boutique. If you plan for this long term, you can take some of the net cash flow from your online and income from other streams of revenue to save for the eventuality of opening a brick and mortar location. Don't bite off more than you can chew. It's better to start small and grow than try to swim the ocean and drown.

As an organization, you must decide what image you want to present. Do you want a more boutique classy look or a full bargain hunting look? Whichever you decide, don't forget to have clear walkways in your store and make shopping fun not dangerous with trip hazards and dirty merchandise.

Here are <u>the basics needs</u> and <u>associated costs</u> of opening a store:

Location (rent) – Ask donors and business owners about possible free or nearly free locations. Property owners can take a tax write-off for donated rent. You can arrange to pay half of their price perhaps, if they are having trouble filling the space. Or maybe someone has a house in a business district that needs a bit of work and you can exchange repairs for rent. Just don't take on anything too large or complicated like structural issues. Start with a smaller location, if that's all you can find, and grow to a larger location when one is available or you have saved enough funds for more rent. It may be a good idea to find a licensed commercial property real estate agent/broker, especially if they will volunteer their time.

Location points to consider:
- Parking
- Loading/unloading
- Visibility

- Other businesses nearby
- Maintenance
- Security
- Storage

Volunteers – Your store will need staff. Offer half day or full day shifts. Volunteers should commit to the same shift every week, so a regular schedule can be drawn up. At least 2 people should staff each shift for safety and coverage.

Register and credit card processing – Through much experimentation, I have found the least expensive and easiest way is utilizing an iPad and Square payment processing for credit/debit cards. If you can get a donated cash register, use that of course. Better yet, perhaps you can get a donated or gently used iPad. They can be purchased for less than $100. You will also need a cash drawer with a case or cash drawer without a case if you have a desk with a drawer for it to live in. if you go the iPad route. Square provides card scanners to plug into iPads for free, plus a register program for the iPad. Square fees are among the lowest (at this point) in the marketplace. However, your bank may offer you a super deal especially for being a non-profit.

Perhaps you can arrange a great deal with another company in exchange for mention in your newsletter or advertising in your store/office. Bottom line: shop around.

Bank Account – Assumedly your organization already has a bank account. Hopefully you have a bookkeeper or treasurer as well. If not, get them, so income and expenses can be professionally balanced and documented.

Retail Displays – Your store will need shelves, racks, cabinets, etc. These can be found on Craigslist, eBay, and Facebook local selling groups. If you have a lot of large stores in your area, call them up and ask if they are getting rid of retail displays. Offer a donation receipt for their taxes. Post a ISO (in search of) on your Facebook page and Craigslist. Go to garage sales and estate sales.

Tags/Supplies – Sticker tags can be found everywhere. You should have some hanging tags as well for non-stick surfaces. If you plan on selling a large quantity of clothing, you might want to look into getting a tagging gun and barbs, although a paper tag and stapler work well too and break less often. It's all about the image you want to present. You will also need racks and hangers if you sell clothing.

Cleaning Supplies – The basics are glass cleaner, degreaser, bathroom cleaner, Goof-Off, and floor cleaner, dust rags and polishing rags. Metal cleaner is a good idea as well, since silver sells so much better when it sparkles. Brooms, a mop, dustpans and a vacuum; this is a dirty business and no one likes shopping in filth. Really, no one.

Electrical – Test everything possible. Get batteries at the Dollar Store and text items. Include the batteries with the items to sell them for more and faster. Have a power strip conveniently located so people can test things for themselves.

The products pictured are among my favorites.

Front Desk and Back Desk – You will of course need a place for your customers to put their items to be rung up and a place for your register. You will also need a desk in the office for your records, to do deposits, paperwork, etc. Regular desks can be found rather easily, but a retail counter might take a bit of looking. Again, try the places recommended for finding store displays: Craigslist, Facebook, local businesses.

Telephone – All businesses need to be reachable. Landlines are more reliable than cell phones, and cheaper for the most part. You can find cheap land line telephones at garage sales, thrift stores, or in your own donations. Again, shop around for the best prices and options, plans and offers are changing all the time.

Business license – This may be covered by already being a 501(c3) but check with your city and county for their specific regulations.

Insurance – Liability and workers' compensation and protection against loss such as if your store should burn down or someone drives through your window. Hey, it happens. Check with your landlord about what his property insurance covers.

TIP: Before you open, visit other thrift stores in the area. Note how many there are. Also note what you like and dislike about how each store is arranged, its displays, tagging, etc. Get ideas about what to do and what NOT to do.

Lastly, but NOT least, you need a name for your store. Since it is supporting your organization and its mission, your store name will be part of your organization's name, such as Humane Society of Smith County Thrift Store.

Here is a great cash register I have used at a lot of nonprofit thrift stores. I really like it because it has a receipt for the customer, but also has a separate roll that keeps a record of every sale, drawer open, etc. that can be used to balance and verify by your manager and bookkeeper. You can also program special keys to track certain sales departments and streams of revenue. It is easy to use and includes a cash drawer for a pretty low price:

https://amzn.to/2UJN8mW

Here is paper for it, 50 rolls for less than 20 dollars:

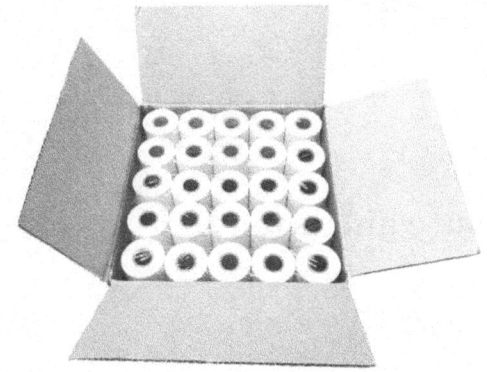

https://amzn.to/2UO2s1G

You can also find rolls of paper at Staples if it's an emergency but they are more $$.

https://amzn.to/2UNH9gY

You need a lighted, flashing sign (street window) and a printed sign (below the lighted sign or on your front door).

Sign cost: $9.96 Exposure and attention: priceless.
https://amzn.to/2URXnG0

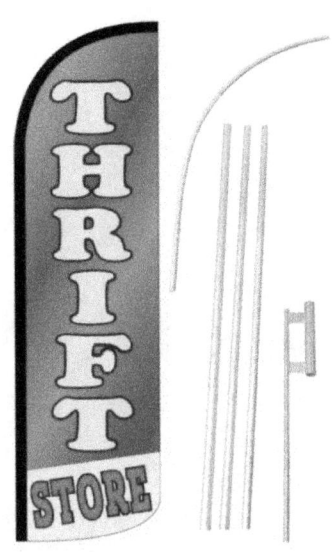

These flags really do make a difference. We saw a 20%+ increase in traffic when we installed just one.

https://amzn.to/2UMcrod

Other Essential Items:
Jewelry scales, magnifying loupe, watch repair kits, ring sizers.

https://amzn.to/2UMehph

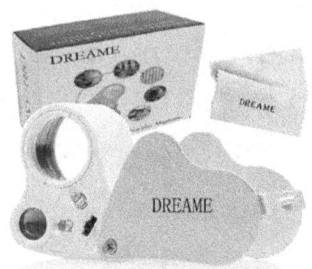

https://amzn.to/2UNdwfx

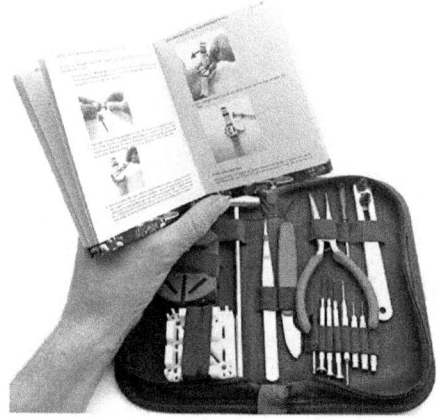

https://amzn.to/2UM2PtY

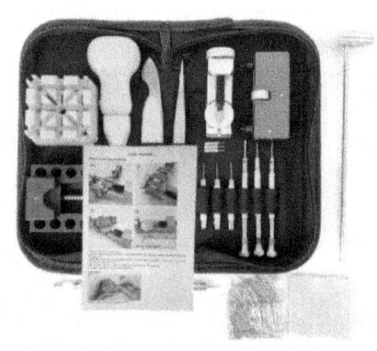

https://amzn.to/2UKWA9K

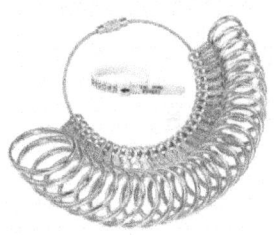

Now let's look at keys to **successful and profitable thrift store operation**.

Inventory Management: Tags should be dated with the month or color coded so staff knows when the item came in and how long it's been there. Depending on size and turnover of merchandise, you can have items go on sale at the 1st of every month, or every 3 weeks, or every 5 or 6 weeks, whatever works best for your store. I have found a 4-6 week rotation works well. So if you're putting things out in March, the items from January would be half price. The items from previous months that have been on sale already, need to be pulled when the sale tag changes. That way you don't end up with too much stock and a cluttered, store that is not conducive to shopping.

Merchandising: You want the store full but not overfull, well stocked but not hard to shop. You don't want customers missing good things because they can't see them!

Dust regularly and wipe off dirty items before putting them out for sale. You don't need to wash them thoroughly, but a good wipe down goes a long way. Windex or all-purpose cleaner is essential. To cut expenses, use old donated washcloths/towels for wiping things down. Then you can wash them every so often and reuse. Have a stock of them in your workroom or office or receiving room. The Dollar Store is a gem for getting cleaning and pricing supplies.

Putting strings of lights along the back of shelves and along window sills looks great, gives light in dark areas, and draws attention from the customer. Mirrors are also great for lightening the displays and highlighting areas or items. Also, a well-placed lamp or three goes a long way when you have dim corners. Makes your store look more open and inviting, and the lamps can be for sale.

Retail Layout: Clear isles to be large enough for someone using a walker or a small stroller or wheelchair.

Make sure your shelving is attractive and sturdy. You can use donated items! Just make sure they look good or get repainted/refurbished.

Cleanliness: Empty trash regularly and recycle everything you can to gut your refuse bill.

Donation Management: Never say anything negative about any donation in front of customers. They may be donors or future donors, unless they hear something negative or offending.

Make sure you have a dedicated 'donation room' or 'receiving area' for incoming donations to be sorted. Have an area designated for unwanted donations. Those items that don't fit your needs or are simply not sellable (broken or in poor condition or don't sell well in your area). It is useful to have a code word for unwanted donations such as 'beach' or 'partner' so you can say 'let's beach this' or 'this goes to the partner area' instead of 'we'll get rid of this' or 'dump this.' It sounds much better to donors or customers who might overhear. Also, it is best to err on the side of caution and take something you don't want (unless it's large furniture you will have to pay to dump) and then dispose of it later when the donor leaves. It only takes a few rejections before words gets around that 'this place doesn't take much of anything.' People are hard to please, so do your best and err on the side of good customer service.

Items you don't want can be taken to other non-profits such as Goodwill, or you can have a trade system with other non-profits who are in a different location. They may sell different items than you, such as furniture and you sell small household items or clothing. You can also take household and clothing items to churches, shelters, and aid organizations.

Pricing: This step can be done at a station in the receiving room or at the front desk, depending on staffing and store layout. It's good to have pricing supplies in both places for efficiency and days with multiple people processing donations. However, if you have a manager, or someone very knowledgeable and fast at sorting, it is a good idea to have 1 or 2 people who do most of the sorting for speed and consistency. If you have multiple people working per day, you can have shelves or bins with price points on them (.50, 1.00, 1.50, 2.00, etc.) and the sorter can sort and the person at the front desk can tag and display items. This provides an efficient way to get a lot of product on the floor and gone through out of your receiving room! Some days, such as end of year and summer, when donations will seem overwhelming, speed is essential.

If you are uncertain how to price, think about garage sale prices, and price about twice that. Or visit other thrift stores such as St. Vincent's or Salvation Army or other small shops in your area to see how they price.

In a nutshell: Price high enough to ensure you are fundraising, but low enough that customers want to purchase items and maintain your reputation for bargains.

- Price stickers should be placed on the item in a location that will not damage the item. For books, place the price sticker on the back of the book. Try to put price stickers on the bottom of items, such as plates and other similar objects.
- Volunteers/Employees should not price items they are intending to purchase. Have

a second, nonbiased employee/volunteer price the item.

- SELF BENEFITING – Remind yourself we are here to benefit the mission of the organization – not ourselves. Price according to the best interest of the organization and fundraising for its mission.

Here are some pricing/value guides to get you started:
https://www.goodwill.org/wp-content/uploads/2010/12/donation_valuation_guide.pdf

https://www.svdpcincinnati.org/userfiles/SVdP_DonorValuationGuide_9-08.pdf

https://satruck.org/Home/DonationValueGuide

Quality control is very important. Electrical and mechanical items should be tested if possible. Store credit can be given for items that can not be fully tested if they don't work when the customer gets them home.

DVDs and CDs should be examined for scratching and those that look 'rough' should not be put out for sale. They won't sell anyway.

Items should be at least wiped off if they are dusty or have food, grease or dirt on them.

Potentially dangerous items should be avoided, such as household chemicals, and sharp/pointy items like knives should be kept in a glass case. Caution: many children's items have had safety recalls. Before selling any of these items, check the Consumer Product Safety Commission website for recalls www.cpsc.gov. They also have a thrift store/reselling guide you should have on hand. They can be ordered free.

It is very appealing to have a senior day discount of 10%-20% one day a week. Choose the 'senior' age (usually 60 or 65) and spread the word.

Gift certificates are great to offer, especially around the holidays. They can also be offered in exchange for something that did not work properly, or a loyal customer who wants to exchange something and you don't want to risk offending them.

Essential References:

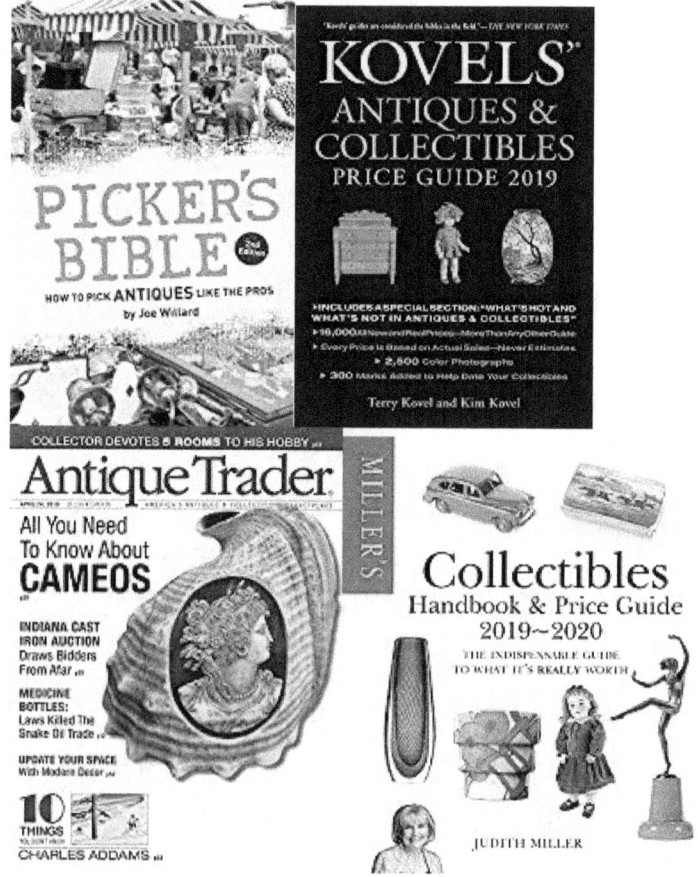

Items with Potentially Higher Value

Belt Buckles

The buckles you want to look for are limited editions (look on the back), pewter/silver/precious metals or stones inlaid, advertising, military, sport teams, sports such as rodeo and racing, and advertising a product or company, artisan crafted especially American Indian.

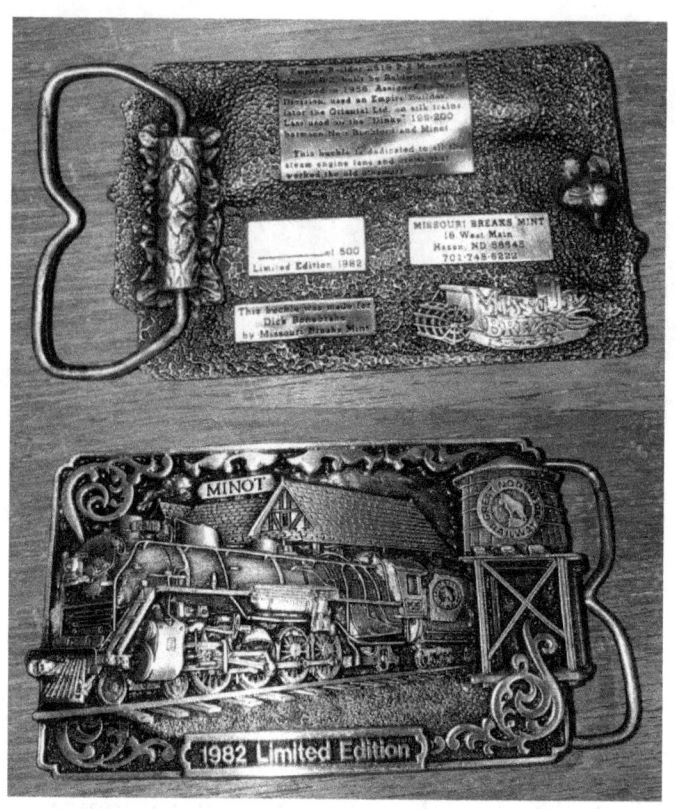

Limited edition pewter buckle featuring railroad.
Sold for $25 in 2019.

Special edition sports team buckle sold for $40 in 2019.

Baskets

Longaberger should be looked up online if it's a large or unusual; basket, otherwise priced 10-15.

Most of the baskets you'll see will be modern mass-produced and not worth your attention. However, for estates and other donations that may hold antique baskets, you need to know what to look for.

Let's start with the basics of baskets:

There are two types of baskets: work and fancy. Working baskets were durably made for a particular purpose, such as egg gathering, apples and other fruits, herb gathering, winnowing, storage, etc. Fancy baskets were those made as a gift or for tourists, with embellishments such as silk ribbon, shells, paint, carving, etc.

Classified into four types, according to Catherine Erdly via Wikipedia:

"Coiled" basketry

uses grasses and rushes

"Plaiting" basketry

uses materials that are wide and braid like: palms, yucca or New Zealand flax

"Twining" basketry

uses materials from roots and tree bark. Twining actually refers to a weaving technique where two or more flexible weaving elements ("weavers") cross each other as they weave through the stiffer radial spokes.

"Wicker" and "Splint" basketry

uses reed, cane, willow, oak, and ash

Modern baskets are often lighter than antique baskets, and do not show the intricate workmanship and wear of an old basket.

Parts of a basket:
- Base (woven splint or solid piece of wood)
- side walls (*spokes, stakes, standards* or *staves* for the frame then the *weavers* or *splint* are woven between) Weavers are usually narrow where splint is usually wide.
- Rim (usually a thicker strip of wood rounded once or twice then single wrapped or double (X) wrapped)

- Handle – swing/drop/bail (moveable) or grip (stationary)
- Lid – sometimes but not always, depending on the intended use of the basket.
- Runners – Usually 2 but up to 4 wood strips on the bottom of the basket for lift (air circulation) and strength.

Early 20th C Basket, possibly Shaker about $50
Note the ageing of the nails/staples, the stains and patina of the wood.

Buttons

There are 2 types of buttons: sew-through with holes for the thread, and shank, with a loop for the thread.

There are 4 sizes:

Diminutive – up to 3/8"

Small – 3/8 to ¾"

Medium – ¾ to 1 ¼"

Large – 1 ¼" and larger

Most buttons aren't worth more than a couple dollars. Batch them in an old glass jar or tin and sell them for $5-10 depending on size of lot and quality. HOWEVER, look through all buttons first and make sure you don't have any of the following:

Jasperware – A fine ceramic/porcelain in light green or blue with white decoration. Often signed on rear by artist.

Buttons on pictorial cards and/or sets of circus, animal, fun shapes

American Indian theme

Hand painted porcelain or glass with unusual picture

Military

Silver (sterling or 800, look for hallmarks)

Satsuma Japanese pottery buttons

Buttons made before 1900

Famous children's book characters

Art glass 'paperweight' buttons

Buttons with specific cities on them such as San Francisco Fire Department

TIP: Search eBay under collectibles and/or antiques for 'button' then choose 'Sewing' and 'Militaria' and 'Antiques' and sort completed auctions by most expensive. You'll see some mind blowing items. You'll also see items that are not related but educational as well.

You can also search any of the terms in the above list of buttons to look for.

Clothing

Pendleton items new or old are valuable, especially the blankets.
Pants and cotton shirts not so much (Good for consignment store), but wool shirts, blazers, skirts, anything plaid, wallets and other accessories all sell well online.

Dooney and Bourke handbags, wallets, organizers, anything with their signature and Duck on it. Items should be in new or like new condition with minimal wear and looking very attractive.

Military – Anything Vietnam war and earlier.

Look for:

- Made in England, Scotland, New York and Paris.
- Items made of Silk, wool, angora, and cashmere
- You can't list Chanel, or other huge designer names that have been copied. Sadly the pirate market has ruined resale for those items unless you are the original owner and can provide a sales receipt of the original purchase showing authenticity.
- Unusual prints or designs

Ben Sherman Pin Up Girl Shirt sold for $35 in 2019

. Coogi Australia Wavy Mercerized Cotton Sweaters sell for $75 and up

Sports teams! Especially new with tag. These socks sold for $10 in 2019

l'artiste By Spring Step Live Ankle Boot Black Leather Multi Tapestry NEW

Sold for $50 in 2019

Electrical

Vintage electronics are rapidly growing in value and desirability.

- 1980's and 90's Walkmans (selling for $10 and up online)
- As new unused VHS tapes and cassette tapes
- 1980's 'boom boxes' (radio and tape portable combination)
- Vintage Game Consoles: Apple, Atari, Commodore, Nintendo
- Vintage light fixtures – especially mid-century (1940's through the 70's)
- Film projectors and reel to reel
- Cameras
- Transistor and countertop radios
- Record players and phonographs
- Computers from the 1980's and early 90's
- Car stereos
- Printers
- Sound equipment from the 70's-80's like amps, synthesizers, stereos and stereo parts, etc.

- Hand Held game systems and cartridges (Nintendo DS, Tetris, Mario, Pac Man, etc.)
- Audio cassettes from the 1970's to mid-1990's in the genres of Punk rock, heavy metal, alternative, acid rock, country rock, rap, hip hop, and ethnic. Must be complete with case and liner (paper with pictures and lyrics). Most classical, and movie soundtracks are not worth anything. A collection of a certain artist or genre are almost always good, such as David Bowie, from early works to the last produced in cassette form. Especially if the group or artist isn't with us anymore.

The list is extensive so if it's at least 20 years old, give it a closer look and test it. Even if it doesn't work, there are people needing parts or who have parts to fix it.

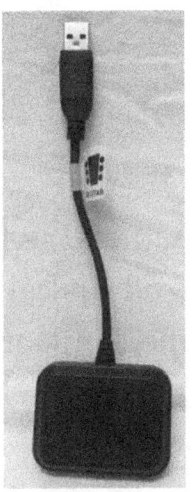

Red Octane Guitar Hero Wireless Receiver for Guitar~ 95451-806~ PS2 PS3

Glass

General: Cobalt blue and ruby red is very popular. Look for art glass pieces that are signed. Fire King, vintage Corning Ware, Pyrex, patterned glass, unusual bottles, etc. Avoid punch sets! I sell maybe 2 a year but see them constantly.

Kitchen glassware from the 1930's-1970's is quite popular. Transfers and designs need to be bright and not faded or scratched.

Anything in Jadeite (opaque light green) is desirable.

Milk glass (opaque white glass) is for the most part flat right now. Covered dishes with animals or figures on them are an exception, or animal pitchers.

Most **bottles** you see won't be worth more than a dollar or two. However, there are some types of bottles you want to keep an eye out for and research to sell online or at least price for more in your store or rummage sales.

Learn the difference between machine made and mouth blown bottles. The first will have mold marks (line up each side) and flat stamped bottom. The blown ones will have a pontil (where the rod was broken off after blowing) which may be rough or polished. They may also have an indented bottom where it was smoothed after blowing.

Free blown bottles were made to 1860. Mold blown were made to about 1903 when the first automatic bottle making machine was invented.

The common way to date a bottle if with mold seams. Bottles before 1860 have mold seams that end low on the neck or at the shoulder. Between 1860 and 1880 the mold seam stops right below the mouth, indicating where the lip was formed or applied separately by hand. Around 1880 the closed mold (full bottle to lip/top) was introduced and the seam ends within a quarter inch of the top. After 1900 the seam goes all the way through the lip.

Colors for bottles are:

Common: Clear, aqua, amber.

Average: Milk glass (opaque white), green, black, olive green.

Rare colors: Teal blue, cobalt, purple/amethyst, yellow, yellow-green, puce.

Plain (no label and no or minimal embossing) rectangular bottles of unknown antique origin are not worth more than a couple dollars apiece. Shaped, embossed, intact paper labels, colored glass, are what you want to look for.

http://www.antiquebottles.com/

https://www.collectorsweekly.com/bottles/fruit-jars

The following guides cover most of what you'll see.

Art glass signatures:

The round spot in the middle is the pontil. It can be rough or polished.

Examples of art glass signatures.

Holiday (Vintage)

Items to look for:

Old World Christmas ornaments (they have a metal tag with OWC or a star shaped hook holder)

Christopher Radko

Limoges

Department 56 (Snowbabies, etc.)

Hallmark (in boxes, look them up, some are better than others)

Polonaise

Slavic Treasures

Lenox

Patricia Breen

Lladro

Danbury Mint

Napco

Norman Rockwell

Any old glass ornaments, especially figures

Vintage paper cut out window/wall pictures

Papier Mache items

Vintage rhinestone holiday jewelry

Hot Wheels

Hot wheels, produced by Mattel Inc. started in 1968. The ones you want to look for are the 'Red Lines' so named because they have a red line around the tires (like a white wall but red). Redlines were produced 1968-1977 and are really the only ones worth anything outside of original packaging. If they are in the original package and the package and the vehicle are in mint or excellent condition (that means hardly any wear to no wear at all like new) then they can go for thousands of dollars. Outside of their original package they can still be valuable and desirable if the paint is not badly chipped, all parts are intact, decals are bright and not worn, etc. If the paint is worn, parts are broken or missing, there is rust, etc. the car is not worth anything.

Lesney Matchbox Toys

Not to be confused with Hot Wheels. From 1947 to 1953, the toys were marked only Lesney England. The 'Matchbox' name came in 1954 but was not part of the mark on the vehicles' undercarriage until the early 1960's.

Any tin or cast toy marked Lesney or Matchbox that is vintage, should be researched.

All cars produced 1947-1983 are marked Made in England or England, and those are the ones you want to look for in good condition.

Linen

- Mid century tea/kitchen towels in bright prints are popular. Animals, children, black Americana, lovely flowers, psychedelic, etc.
- Vintage chenille! Look for the sewn back not plastic or rubber or finished backs.
- Hooked rugs and seat covers and wall hangings.

- Needlework pictures.
- Rag rugs are always popular.
- Hand made quilts of any age, especially old ones.
- Patchwork anything.
- Vintage complete sheet sets in good gently used condition from the 1970's and earlier, and children's sets with popular characters (like care Bears, Disney, sci-fi, etc.) from the 90's and earlier.
- Lace tablecloths, clothes, unusual items like collars. The more intricate the better.
- Vintage sewing, needlepoint, cross stitch, or similar sets that are unused.

Mid-Century table cloths

Patchwork quilt $65

Marbles

Marbles can be a lot of fun and bring good value. Looks for pontils (where the rod was attached while forming the molten glass), this indicates a handmade marble, usually dating to before 1900. There are modern art glass marbles as well, which are quite desirable, look for a signature. Common marbles such as Cat's Eyes, two-color patch and ribbon marbles can be bunched together in an old jar and sold for $10-25 depending on the size and condition of the jar and marbles.

2 signed art glass marbles$20 each

Mid-Century Items

Items produced in the 1940's-1970's are very popular with millennials, gen-Xers and decorators today. Lamps, Mid-Century Modern style items, hook yarn wall hangings or rugs, macramé, floral prints, 1950's colors (pink, mauve, black, chrome, teal), 1960's-70's colors (burnt orange, avocado green, rust/red, yellow, and those dismal browns), mushrooms, lamp tables, record cabinets, etc.

If you grew up with it or your parents did, it's probably something that's coming back now.

Franciscan VINTAGE Atomic Starburst 15" Oval Serving Dish Mid Century Modern

Sold for $20 in 2019

Mid Century Modern Jo Wallis Table Lamp w/ Birch Bark Lamp Shade ~ Atomic $65

Pez

Here is the rule of thumb for Pez: No feet.

The earliest dispensers were called Pez Regulars and do not have a head but look like Bic lighters. The reproductions have curved heads, the old ones have a thumb crest in the front like a tiara or rooster. The old ones are rare and desirable.

Most dispensers worth anything are the early models without feet. There are some exceptions:

Baseball Set (glove and ball head, bat and home run plate), Barney Bear, Bambi, Batman (blue or black w/ short ears), Bride and Groom set, Charlie Brown with closed eyes, Chip (of Chip and Dale but Dale was not produced. Looks like a critter in a black hat.), Cool Cat, Droopy with moveable ears, Dumbo, Foghorn Leghorm, Henry Hawk, King Louie (ape from Jungle Book), Lil Bad Wolf (looks like a black and white cat really), Lucy with white around her eyes or features in white, Mimic Monkey (with ball cap), Mowgli (boy with chin-length hair), Olympic Vucko Wolves (Olympic rings on back of head), One Eyed Monster, Peter Pez Clown with Rico hat, Petunia Pig, Pif the Dog (yellow head with big nose and PIF on left ear), Play World Sets complete on card, Practical Pig (with hat), Raven (with glasses), Roadrunner, Thumper Bunny, Tyke (puppy dog), Wile E Coyote, Zinniafant (elephant).

If it is a holiday dispenser on the original card, it may be scarce as they were short runs for that particular holiday.

Also look for the Full Body Robot and Santa dispensers. They were the only ones produced in full body.

Plastic bags with add little to no values.

Whistle dispensers are good: Dog, Duck, Frog, Indian (American), Lamb, Monkey, Owl, Panda (with removable eyes), Pig, Rooster.

Make sure the head pulls back smoothly and springs back when released. If it flops around the spring is broken. Look for melt marks on the stem, cracks, missing parts inside, discoloration. All these reduce value.

Posters

- Rock groups
- Movies
- TV Shows
- Psychedelic art
- Sporting events (rodeos, race car, boxing, etc.)
- Groovy 60's and 70's
- Signed and numbered by hand art lithograph posters
- Educational posters

Must be in good condition with no creases, stains, no tears, and no pin holes. If they have a few tiny edge tears or a couple tiny pin holes but will still look good framed, then research it.

1980's TV shows such as Miami Vice original posters from about $20 currently.

I recently sold a set of astronomical posters, five made to span a wall, for $30, and a vintage illustrated history timeline for $10.

Adams Synchrological Chart/Map of History on 5 Posters sold for

$20

Sewing & Craft

Buttons – See the Buttons category earlier

Yarn – Wool, merino, hand dyed, Alpaca, and other artisan or high end yarns. If you get 2 or more skeins of the same color, list them online because someone will need that color and many are discontinued and bring more on the secondary market.

Thread – Sell individual spools of thread for .25 modern (plastic spools) .50 vintage (wooden spools) or sell them in lots online.

Fabric – Vintage sell online. If they aren't enough for online: large pieces price $1-5 depending on yardage and quality/pattern, small pieces cut into quilt squares or rug making strips and bundle for a few dollars.

Notions and Tools – Lot them online or price them $1-2 each depending on what they are.

Here is an example of vintage craft tools and notions that sold online for $30:

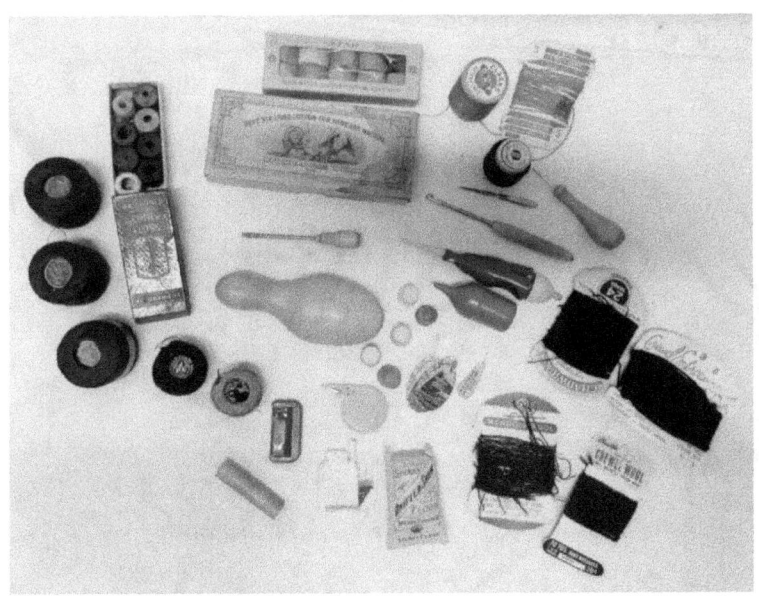

Lot of Hand Crafted Yarns - Wool, Cashmere, Alpaca sold for $84

Snap Back Caps

Also called trucker caps and mesh back caps. The ones from the 1980's and earlier are usually the most desirable. They are baseball style caps that have an adjustable strap in the back with pegs and holes to adjust the size and fit, thus the 'snap back' name.

The front will be padded with transfer decal or embroidered design. They can be nylon, leather, corduroy or denim most commonly. I have seen a single hat sell for $300 and a group of dirty, abused caps go for $450.

The types of snap back hats are:

caps sold at truck stops advertising machinery, local companies, parts suppliers, auto companies, etc.

Sports caps with team names

Music merchandise with a band or artist logo

Military – Navy, Army, Marines, Air Force, National Guard, a unit or ship or division.

The ones to look for are John Deere, Mack Truck, Harley Davidson, famous rock groups especially those now defunct or early caps of legendary groups and artists such as KISS, Rolling Stones, David Bowie, Michael Jackson, etc.

These are easy to research online. Just search snap back cap and whatever is on the cap.

Tools

Most tools you will see will be the run-of-the-mill much-used screwdrivers and plyers, but occasionally you may get something worth researching. For tools you want to research anything that is old or unusual. Leather working or firearms tools, tools with wooden handles, technical tools like surveying equipment and scientific calipers, and brass tools.

Good condition modern tools such as power tools or Craftsman, Stalney, Keen Kutter, and other good brands should be looked up as well. Verify they work before selling them.

Keep in mind that 'worn out' tools can often be cleaned up and used for craft and repurpose projects and can bring a few dollars just for that.

Toys

If it's new in package or new with tag, research it.

If it's a pop culture related toy, (TV show, movie, music, etc.) research it.

Disney vintage (1990 and earlier) are worth looking into.

LEGOS – Sets (look them up) or individual pieces in a sandwich baggie for $5

McDonald's toys if they are 1980's or earlier and in good condition.

Transformers: Made by Hasbro. Generation One 1984-1990 are most valuable.

Series 1 1984 has no heat sensitive 'rubsigns' , just red and silver 'faction' (Autobot or Decepticon) labels.

Series 2 – 1985 has heat sensitive 'rubsigns' which are decals that show faction when finger is pressed to them, like a mood ring.

Always test battery operated toys. Use dollar store batteries and include them with the toy. You can get much better selling and price results. If it's really obnoxious, price it cheap and an aunt, uncle, or grandparent will buy it with vengeful intentions.

Vintage 1977 Kenner Star Wars 3.75" Chewbacca
Action Figure Made in Hong Kong

Sold for $9.50 in 2019

2010 WWE Wrestling Mattel Elite Legends
Series 2 The Iron Sheik Figure

Sold for $18 in 2019

Antique Cast Iron Metal Ram Sheep Toy Collectible Painted Small Figurine Sold for $25

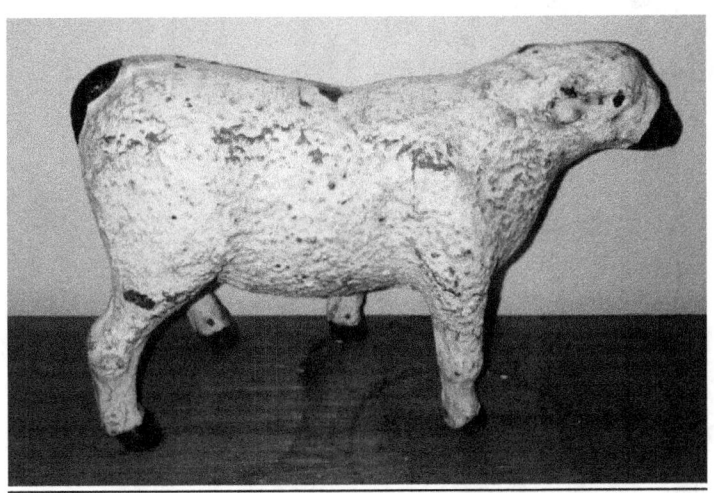

VHS Tapes

Youth of the 1980's rejoice! VHS is making a comeback, they are even making VHS players again. Most VHS tapes aren't worth more than fifty cents, but there are some exceptions:

THE DARK PLANET (1989)

OUT OF THE BOX (1998-2004) Disney pre-school series, especially the holiday ones.

THE PROWLER (1981) Oversized "big box" version most valuable selling for a few hundred, while the standard cardboard edition sells for over $50.

TAMMY AND THE T-REX (1994)

DEADLY PREY (1987)

BLOOD LAKE (1987)

BARNEY (1992-2009)

PROFESSIONAL WRESTLING TAPES

STAR WARS (1977) Original 1980's version before the edits and additions.

A HISTORY OF VIOLENCE (2005) Last major studio movie to be released on VHS.

DONNA SUMMER A HOT SUMMER NIGHT (1986)

TERROR OF BLOOD GYM (1995)

EMMET OTTER'S JUG BAND CHRISTMAS MUPPETS (1985)

TEXAS CHAINSAW MASSACRE ~ ASTRAL VIDEO - 85 MINUTES (1980'S)

THE TEXAS CHAINSAW MASSACRE ~ FILMWAYS ~ (1984)

THE GOONIES (1985)

Cheesy horror and sci-fi movies from the 1980's and 1990's should always be researched. Many had limited releases and are very collectible these days.

Disney Movies like new in clamshell cases or new in shrink-wrap. Especially the 'Black Diamond Editions' which have a diamond logo on the spines.

To find out what's valuable without searching each movie you receive, go to EBay and click SHOP BY CATEGORY then DVDs & MOVIES then VHS TAPES then look at what's selling under the $10-35 and Over $35 prices, sorted by most expensive to least. Don't forget to check the Completed Items to see what sold and what didn't.

For Etsy search VHS then sort by HIGHEST PRICE (top right corner of results.) Sadly you can't search completed listings and see what sold, which Etsy should really change.

Google: Search VHS RARE and click the SHOPPING tab to choose the results with items for sale.

Free Willy 2: The Adventure Home Sealed w/ Mystical Whale Pendant Sold for $17

Other Really Useful Stuff

Great general sites and guides for collectibles/antiques:

https://antique-marks.com/ - great marks resource

www.kovels,com – Everything antiques and collectibles

https://www.1stdibs.com/ - high end collectibles and art

https://www.proxibid.com/ - auctions galore

https://www.estatesales.net/ - Find estate sales by location, then ask them for leftovers!

https://garagesalefinder.com/

https://www.liveauctioneers.com/ - more auctions

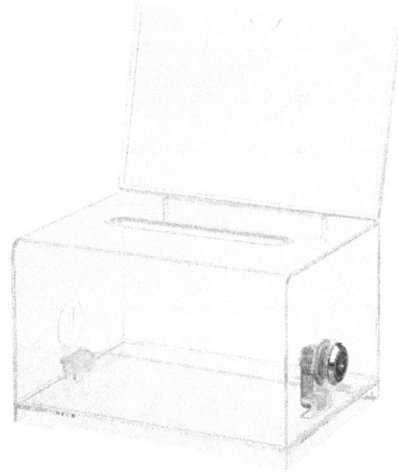

Don't forget the donation box!

Have a donation box on the counter in

Getting an e-mail is important so you can send your donors your monthly newsletter to keep your organization in their mind for donations.
Example of donation form:

YOUR LOGO HERE
your organization name here
is a 501(c)3 Non-Profit Organization Tax ID: XX-XXXXXX

Date: _____

Name:_____

Business/Agency:_____

Address:_____

City:_____

Zip: _____ Phone:_____

Email Address:

Item	Estimated Value

Thank you for your generosity!

_____

Signature of Staff Receiving Donation

For your donation form, you can have 2 part carbon copies printed (top customer fills out and bottom copy is carbon for the customer, usually white and yellow) or you can just use regular printer paper and print your own and copy each one when the customer fills it out.

For more choices:
https://www.google.com/search?source=hp&ei=ba YEXOzrINbC0PEP4amWmAE&q=in+kind+donat ion+form+example&oq=in+kind+donation+form& gs_l=psy-ab.1.2.0l4j0i22i30l6.854.4194..6946...0.0..0.86.119 8.21......0....1..gws-wiz.....0..0i131.N5A5VNPtN_c

Always keep a copy of the donation form and have a database of donors, which can be used for marketing, thank you notes, holiday cards, fundraising ask letters or invitations, etc.

You do not fill in the value of the items, the donor does that. Here are the IRS guidelines:

Fair market value is the price at which property would change hands between a willing buyer and a willing seller, neither having to buy or sell, and both having reasonable knowledge of all the relevant facts.

Used clothing: The fair market value of used clothing and other personal items is usually far less than the price you paid for them. There are no fixed formulas or methods for finding the value of items of clothing. You should claim as the value the price that buyers of used items actually pay in used clothing stores, such as consignment or thrift shops.

Example: Kristin donated a coat to a thrift store operated by her church. She paid $300 for the coat 3 years ago. Similar coats in the thrift store sell for $50. The fair market value of the coat is $50. Kristin's donation is limited to $50.

*Bottom line, for most items, value the item at what you the receiving organization will sell it for.

Concerning valuable and/or collectible items, here is a link to the IRS publication 561: https://www.irs.gov/pub/irs-pdf/p561.pdf

Additional information can be found at https://www.irs.gov under Credits & Deductions.

Here are pricing guides for the 3 major thrift retailers. If you want to go above and beyond, you can print them for your customers or have a sheet with the online addresses.

https://www.goodwill.org/wp-content/uploads/2010/12/donation_valuation_guide.pdf

https://www.svdpcincinnati.org/userfiles/SVdP_DonorValuationGuide_9-08.pdf

https://satruck.org/Home/DonationValueGuide

Key Websites for dealers and collectors:

http://www.etsy.com

http://eBay.com

http://www.collectorscorner.com/

https://www.collectorsweekly.com/

https://www.kovels.com/

https://www.antiquetrader.com/

http://journalofantiques.com/

To contact me:

Please post a review on Amazon for me, and let me know of any additions, clarifications, or suggestions.

https://www.etsy.com/shop/TheCutetique

Homeward Bound Pets EBay Store:

https://www.ebay.com/str/homewardboundthriftshop

At Homeward Bound Pets Thrift Shop we offer a variety of useful, collectible, or even delightfully eclectic (most recently, a handmade Mikhael Gorbachev Christmas tree ornament) items. Our store features both new and gently used items from antique to vintage to modern in age. We have books, art, jewelry, home decor, kitchen items, china, videos, music, video games, electronics, and pet supplies are just a short list of the many wonderful things you'll find throughout the "aisles" of our store. But, the very best part is knowing, as you shop our store, that 100% of the proceeds from each item you buy will go to help homeless cats and dogs, kittens and puppies at Oregon's first no-kill shelter! That's right, we are a 501(c)(3) nonprofit that opened in 1975 and we continue to help animals find new furever homes throughout the Yamhill County area today.

If you would be so kind, would you take a moment to leave a review on Amazon and/or Goodreads for this book?

Just a note on the links I provide: Yes, they are affiliate links and I get a small kickback if you purchase something. However, I never recommend something I have not used myself and found extremely helpful. All the items I recommend I really love. If you do not want to use the affiliate link I provide, no problem, just go directly to Amazon or EBay and purchase. I will never know.

www.ingramcontent.com/pod-product-compliance
Lightning Source LLC
Chambersburg PA
CBHW070936180526
45158CB00023B/1470